Lent, 2002

+ Dale,

Here is
some Lenten reading
for you -- good to
be with you in Florida.

Peace,

Bob

Ashes
TO
Easter

Ashes
TO
Easter

LENTEN MEDITATIONS

Robert F. Morneau

A Crossroad Book
The Crossroad Publishing Company
New York

"Hidden Treasure" by Sr. Maria Corona Crumback, I.H.M.,
first appeared in *Review for Religious* 52 (1993): 460.

1996

The Crossroad Publishing Company
370 Lexington Avenue, New York, NY 10017

Printed in the United States of America

Library of Congress Cataloging-in-Publication Data

Morneau, Robert F., 1938-
  Ashes to Easter : Lenten meditations / Robert F. Morneau.
    p. cm.
  Includes bibliographical references.
  ISBN 0-8245-1564-1
    1. Lent–Meditations. 2. Devotional calendars–Catholic Church.
  3. Catholic Church–Prayer-books and devotions–English. I. Title.
BX2170.L4M68 1996
242'.34–dc20   95-45166
                                                       CIP

Contents

PREFACE

Douglas Steere, one of the great Quakers of the twentieth century, once stated: "To pray is to pay attention to the deepest thing that we know."[1] Lent is a time of paying attention, being alert to the stirrings of the Spirit, hearing the cry of the poor, being respectful of our own inner voices.

There are certain people who are especially gifted in helping us pay attention, indeed, to be prayerful people. Prophets are in this category as are some parents and teachers. And then there are the poets, the users of language in intense and concentrated form. Lent might be well enriched by traveling with them on a forty day journey.

The great Anglican spiritual writer Evelyn Underhill saw the link between poetry and prayer: "Poetry ever goes like the royal banners before ascending life; therefore man may safely follow its leadership in his prayer, which — or should be — life in its intensest form."[2] Poetry, like prayer, is characterized by intensity, intimacy, and incisiveness. Both lead us toward the truth and beauty, and, hopefully, into the woods of goodness.

As intense forms of communication prayer and poetry speak directly to the life of the soul. It is fitting, therefore, that these two spiritual happenings be brought together during the season of Lent. Poetry often expresses the deepest desires of the soul

---

1. Douglas V. Steere, *Together in Solitude* (New York: Crossroad Publishing Co., 1982), 25.

2. *An Anthology of the Love of God from the Writings of Evelyn Underhill,* ed. Lumsden Barkway and Lucy Menzies (London: Mowbray & Co., 1976), 50.

and gets us in touch with religious longings. Prayer nourishes the greatest treasure that we have, our spiritual lives.

In an excellent study of the poet Gerard Manley Hopkins, Margaret Ellsberg speaks about the relationship between sacramental and poetic language. In Hopkins, both languages focus on the mystery of God:

> Sacramental language and poetic language share certain tasks. The divine manifests itself in concrete things through sacraments; poetry through such devices as symbolism and metaphor condenses an unseen reality into words. For Hopkins, who wished to use poetry to address, reveal, and praise God, poetic words shared the responsibility and power of sacramental words.[3]

Lent is a season to address God in praise and thanksgiving; Lent is a season to expose ourselves to sacramental and poetic revelations of our Lord.

The format for this volume is straightforward: (1) identification of the day of Lent and the Gospel reading (the reader is encouraged to spend a good ten minutes in meditative reading of the Gospel passage); (2) a brief contextual comment on the Gospel; (3) a refrain (antiphon) taken from the Divine Office summarizing a core idea in the Gospel (this can be used as a mantra in one's prayer); (4) a selection of poetry to read out loud and more than once; (5) a commentary on the poem followed by three questions for personal reflection; (6) a concluding prayer taken from the morning prayer of the Divine Office.

Since this volume deals with poetry and prayer, it is fitting that we end this preface with a poem. It is a verse centering upon the Annunciation, a feast day celebrated during Lent. The inspiration for this poem by Sister Maria Corona Crumback, I.H.M,

---

3. Margaret Ellsberg, *Created to Praise: The Language of Gerard Manley Hopkins* (New York: Oxford University Press, 1987), 45.

came from a sculpture done by Sr. Mary M. Paul, I.H.M. The sculpture is entitled *The Handmaid.* A Lenten challenge as we begin this journey: memorize the following poem and etch in your imagination the young, noble maiden who said yes to God.

THE HANDMAID

Is this the way it was —
The ageless salvation gift's announcing
Sculpted in a moment of time?
Strangely different, touching, haunting,
Earthily commonplace, sublimely graced.

She stands — a humble toiler
Strong, queenly, poised.
Head turned, stilled with surprise
At the breath of angel voice.
Eyes and mouth resolute
Yet mellowed warm with winsome tenderness.
Budding breasts revealing her readiness for birth.

Cloak and girdled-gown, their wind-brushed flowing
Clasped in a hand that would let
No hindrance to the message,
Even here where she toils gathering wheat.
Feet firmly resting on God's good earth
Yearning in wait for its saviour.

A total, human woman:
   "How can this be ...?
A total, open servant:
   "Be it done unto me ..."

The wait is over
And WORD becomes flesh.

This Yahweh-woman
Stands forever on wheat:
Totally His, handmaid and mother,
Yet, gift to His people,
One of our own.

Sr. Maria Corona Crumback, I.H.M.

Ashes
TO
Easter

ASH WEDNESDAY
Matthew 6:1–6, 16–18

T HE SEASON of Lent is about discipleship — following the way of Jesus. The Lord, our "master beggar," instructs us in the values of the Gospel: prayer (ordering our relationship with God), fasting (getting our own house in order), almsgiving (reaching out to our sisters and brothers). Jesus reminds us that the manner in which we do these spiritual exercises, in secret and for God's glory, is as important as what we do.

Refrain: "When you fast, do not put on a gloomy face, like the hypocrites."

THE MASTER BEGGAR

Worse than the poorest mendicant alive,
the pencil man, the blind man with his breath
of music shaming all who do not give,
are You to me, Jesus of Nazareth.

Must You take up Your post on every block
of every street? Do I have no release?
Is there no room of earth that I can lock
to Your sad face, Your pitiful whisper "Please"?

I seek the counters of time's gleaming store
but make no purchases, for You are there.
How can I waste one coin while You implore
with tear-soiled cheeks and dark blood-matted hair?

And when I offer You in charity
pennies minted by love, still, still You stand
fixing Your sorrowful wide eyes on me.
Must all my purse be emptied in Your hand?

Jesus, my beggar, what would You have of me?
Father and mother? the lover I longed to know?
The child I would have cherished tenderly?
Even the blood that through my heart's valves flow?

I too would be a beggar. Long tormented,
I dream to grant You all and stand apart
with You on some bleak corner, tear-frequented,
and trouble mankind for its human heart.

Jessica Powers

The great questions of life deal with our finitude, our guilt, our anxiety, our death. These must be courageously and vigorously addressed. As Christians we have yet another, central question — who do we say Jesus is? It is a question that Jesus himself posed to the first disciples.

Each person and every generation must answer this query. Sometimes the answers are startling. The poet Jessica Powers describes her experience of Jesus as someone beneath the poorest beggar, the pencil man on the street corner, the blind man shaming us to give with his music.

Here Jesus is demanding and relentless, asking us to give our total self to the work of the kingdom. No wonder many walk away from this Jesus.

1. Where have you met Christ on your faith journey? In church? At the table? On street corners? In shelters?

2. What purchases will you make/not make this Lent?

3. What is the Lord asking you this day to give up: Father? Mother? Lover? Child? Ego?

Praying with the Church

Lord,
protect us in our struggle against evil.
As we begin this discipline of Lent,
make this day holy by our self-denial.
Grant this through our Lord Jesus Christ, your Son,
who lives and reigns with You and the Holy Spirit,
one God, for ever and ever.

THURSDAY after ASH WEDNESDAY
Luke 9:22–25

S UFFERING, rejection, and death were essential ingredients in
the life of Jesus. So too were celebration, loving friendships,
and life-giving encounters. Lent is a season in which we are challenged to integrate this ambiguous journey of faith. It is a season
to learn more deeply the secrets of the paschal mystery. By losing
our lives on the cross, we gain the glory of eternal life.

Refrain: "If anyone wishes to be my disciple, he must deny
himself, take up his cross, and follow me, says the Lord."

THE SIGN OF THE CROSS

The lovers of Christ lift out their hands to
the great gift of suffering.
For how could they seek to be warmed and clothed
and delicately fed

to wallow in praise and to drink deep draughts
of an undeserved affection,
have castle for home and a silken couch for bed,
when He the worthy went forth, wounded and hated,
and grudged of even a place to lay His head?

This is the badge of the friends of the Man of Sorrows:
the mark of the cross, faint replica of His,
become ubiquitous now; it spreads like a wild blossom
on the mountains of time and in each of the crevices.
Oh, seek that land where it grows in a rich abundance
with its thorny stem and its scent like bitter wine,
for wherever Christ walks He casts its seed
and He scatters its purple petals.
It is the flower of His marked elect, and the fruit
it bears is divine.

Choose it, my heart. It is a beautiful sign.

Jessica Powers

One of the crises of our times is the loss of symbols and images
that once gave us a sense of identity and destiny. A central image
was the cross, a sign of God's redemptive love as well as the
tragedy of human sin. As Pope John Paul II eloquently reminds
us, it is a sign of contradiction.

Discipleship, the following of Jesus, demands that the cross
be embraced. Not to trod the path that Jesus walked because of
fear means that we will not share in the glory of his resurrection.
Those who have befriended Christ not only accept the crosses
that come in life; they intentionally seek to embrace the suffering
that is part of the body of Christ. Great courage is needed to visit
the home of a family grieving over suicide, to walk in the slums
of Calcutta, to taste the pain of the terminally ill.

1. Do you consider yourself a friend of "the Man of Sorrows?" Any marks on your soul to verify this friendship?

2. Are the crosses you now carry chosen willingly or borne begrudgingly?

3. Do you see the cross as a "beautiful sign"?

Praying with the Church

Lord,
may everything we do,
begin with your inspiration,
continue with your help,
and reach perfection under your guidance.
We ask this through our Lord Jesus Christ, your Son,
who lives and reigns with You and the Holy Spirit,
one God, for ever and ever.

FRIDAY after ASH WEDNESDAY
Matthew 9:14–15

FASTING can be done for a variety of reasons: to gain liberation from some addiction or vice; to be countercultural, witnessing a different set of values to the dominant culture; to extend compassion in solidarity with those who suffer. Jesus comments on the proper seasons to fast and to feast. Our fasting during Lent helps us to experience the plight of our needy sisters and brothers.

Refrain: "When you meet those who are in need of clothing, do not turn away from them, for they are your brothers. Then your light shall break forth like the dawn, and your good deeds shall go before you."

THE MASSES

My love had not the openness to hold
so cumbersome a human multitude.
People in bulk would turn the dials of my heart to Cold.
The mind would bolt its doors and curtly vow
to leave the crowded streets for a while.
And yet if there were patronage in heaven
my passion was to be
mother of the masses, claiming by some small right of anguish
this piteous and dear humanity.
Out of its need my heart began devising
ways to receive this breathing populace
without the warm oppression of its weight,
and the fastidious mind sought out as good
a multiplicity of motherhood
till the reluctant answer entered late:
I learned from God the ancient primal mother
whose hunger to create has brought forth these,
a multitude in lone nativities,
whose love conceived the numberless, and none
by twos and thousands; and with Him I bear them
in separate tenderness, one by one.

Jessica Powers

"Compassion fatigue" is a current spiritual malady. Overwhelmed by the number of suffering people, confused on how to change systems that recycle poverty and violence, distraught by our limited energy and resources, we are tempted to turn away from our sisters and brothers in need. Why even light a single candle in such vast darkness?

Jesus does not demand more than what is possible. We need but respond as lovingly and as appropriately as we can to the situation at hand. We are not messiahs, but we are servants of the Messiah. Our task is a "separate tenderness," sensing the needy one by one, changing our system through proper social and political channels. Our passionate concern for the masses must find incarnate experience in helping our neighbors, and we need not have to ask who they are.

1. How open is your heart to the masses, the multitudes?

2. Whom does God ask you to help this day, one by one?

3. Do you belong to any network seeking to bring about systematic change for the sake of justice?

Praying with the Church

Lord,
with your loving care,
guide the penance we have begun.
Help us to persevere with love and sincerity.
Grant this through our Lord Jesus Christ, your Son,
who lives and reigns with You and the Holy Spirit,
one God, for ever and ever.

SATURDAY after ASH WEDNESDAY
Luke 5:27–32

WHERE does heaven happen? We might ask Levi this question, a person who sat at table with the Lord Jesus. Heaven has to do with eating and drinking at the banquet of God. And, a surprise, many strange guests are invited — even you and I!

Refrain: "Store up for yourself treasures in heaven where neither rust nor moth can destroy."

HEAVEN

The gates of heaven are an allegory
and only symbol shapes its guarded door,
nor does the soul plunge headlong into glory
without a rumor of a light before.

Though God, indeed, has reservoirs of morning
whose unguessed joy we distantly extol,
yet word and choice are altering and adorning:
heaven is something happening in the soul.

Jessica Powers

Heaven happens in the soul. It is there that we encounter God in unique ways. There darkness yields to light; there sadness gives way to "unguessed joy"; there even our failures are transformed into strange glories.

What is the gateway to heaven? How do we enter? Some might claim moral righteousness gives us entry to the divine presence. We merit heaven by good deeds. Levi knew otherwise. The gates of heaven are God's mercy and love.

1. What is happening in your soul these first four days of Lent?

2. Is your treasure rust-proof or not?

3. Who sits at your table? Is it a heavenly experience?

Praying with the Church

Father,
look upon our weakness
and reach out to help us with your loving power.
We ask this through our Lord Jesus Christ, your Son
who lives and reigns with You and the Holy Spirit,
one God, for ever and ever.

First Week of Lent

FIRST SUNDAY of LENT

Matthew 4:1–11 (A); Matthew 1:12–15 (B);
Luke 4:1–13 (C)

S OMEONE once said that the two major metaphors of life are the garden and the river. Surely, these images speak eloquently of what are our lives all about. But another image is central to our human existence, biblical in character, realistic in so many ways. It is the metaphor of the desert. In this apparently barren land we struggle with the demons that confront us, seeking to establish our true freedom and remain true to our identity. Jesus models this struggle for us. But a fourth image comes to mind: the moor — yet another piece of geography that speaks of the sacred, of transcendence. Perhaps Emerson was right when he maintained that "here is best," be it Eden or the Nile, the Sahara or some lonely British moor.

Refrain: "Jesus was led by the Spirit into the desert to be tempted by the devil; and when he had fasted for forty days and forty nights, he was hungry."

The Moor

I entered it on soft foot,
Breath held like a cap in the hand.
It was quiet.
What God was there made himself felt,
Not listened to, in clean colours
That brought a moistening of the eye,
In movement of the wind over grass.

There were no prayers said. But stillness
Of the heart's passion — that was praise
Enough; and the mind's cession
Of its kingdom. I walked on,
Simple and poor, while the air crumbled
And broke on me generously as bread.

R. S. Thomas

To walk the moor, to tend the garden, to sit still by the river, to battle temptations in the desert — wherever we are at any given time can be like a church to us. God is near, sometimes heard, more often felt. If our hearts are filled with awe (cap in hand) and our minds the silence (it was quiet), our eyes may be moistened by God's holy peace.

Our prayers here might well be nonverbal. It is right and just to give thanks; it is also right and just always and everywhere to praise God by silent attentiveness. To focus on God's kingdom of peace and let go of our narcissism gives glory to God and joy to our souls.

When we embrace simplicity and poverty, graces of inestimable value, our journey through life will be immensely enriched. Bread from heaven, sacramental nourishment, will be bestowed on us in abundance. Then we shall become a eucharistic people, filled with gratitude and eternal thanksgiving.

1. What places are like a church to you? Why?

2. Besides vocal prayer, how else do you pray?

3. Are simplicity and poverty ideals in your Christian life?

Praying with the Church

Father,
through our observance of Lent,
help us to understand the meaning
of your Son's death and resurrection,
and teach us to reflect it in our lives.
Grant this through our Lord Jesus Christ, your Son,
who lives and reigns with you and the Holy Spirit,
one God, for ever and ever.

MONDAY of the FIRST WEEK of LENT
Matthew 25:31–46

THE TWO BOOKENDS of Matthew's Gospel are the Beatitudes (Matt. 5) and the Last Judgment scene (Matt. 25). Here we see the vision and the demands of Jesus. Here are the values and imperatives that give us entrance into the Christian life. God's word leads us down the path of redemption into the mystery of eternal life.

Refrain: "You have been blessed by my Father; come and receive the kingdom prepared for you from the foundation of the world."

REDEMPTION

Having been tenant long to a rich Lord,
  Not thriving, I resolved to be bold,
  And make a suit unto him, to afford
A new small-rented lease, and cancel th' old.

In heaven at his manor I him sought:
  They told me there, that he was lately gone
  About some land, which he had dearly bought
Long since on earth, to take possession.

I straight return'd, and knowing his great birth,
  Sought him accordingly in great resorts;
  In cities, theaters, gardens, parks, and courts:
At length I heard a ragged noise and mirth

  Of thieves and murderers: there I him espied,
  Who straight, Your suit is granted, said, and died.

George Herbert

Where is Jesus to be found? In what places are we to look for him or where should we go to be found? Real estate is not the issue. Rather, we find Christ in the lives of people who have been stripped of all false security, alienating power, narcissistic moods.

The Lenten journey intersects with jail cells, shelters for the homeless, soup kitchens, the smelly halls of nursing homes, the slums behind the stock yards. Christ is also met at the breakfast table, the political discussion, the legal chambers, the concert hall. We need but look and listen with reverence and intensity to discover the concealed presence of our God.

1. What are your favorite haunts? Whom do you find there?

2. Do you find Jesus more on the upper or under side of life?

3. Where does Jesus find you? In what landscapes?

Praying with the Church

God our savior,
bring us back to you
and fill our minds with your wisdom.
May we be enriched by our observance of Lent.
Grant this through our Lord Jesus Christ, your Son,
who lives and reigns with You and the Holy Spirit,
one God, for ever and ever.

TUESDAY of the FIRST WEEK of LENT
Matthew 6:7–15

O N ASH WEDNESDAY we were instructed to do three things:
pray, fast, give alms. Now we are taught by Jesus how to
communicate with his Father. While praying this prayer it might
well happen that the Lord will also instruct us in the ways of
discipline and service.

Refrain: "Lord, teach us to pray as John taught his disciples."

PRAYER (I)

Prayer the Church's banquet, angels' age,
    God's breath in man returning to his birth,
    The soul in paraphrase, heart in pilgrimage,
    The Christian plummet sounding heav'n and earth;

Engine against th' Almighty, sinners' tower,
　　Reversed thunder, Christ-side-piercing spear,
　　The six-days world transposing in an hour,
A kind of tune, which all things hear and fear;

Softness, and peace, and joy, and love, and bliss,
　　Exalted Manna, gladness of the best,
　　Heaven in ordinary, man well drest,
The milky way, the bird of Paradise,

　　Church-bells beyond the stars heard, the soul's blood,
　　The land of spices; something understood.

George Herbert

In prayer we lift our mind and heart to God. In prayer, "reversed thunder," we reach out in praise and thanksgiving, in intercession and sorrow. In prayer we "sound heav'n and earth," knowing that God is the one who invites us into divine mystery.

We need to relearn how to pray. Jesus teaches the apostles and us the essence of prayer in today's Gospel passage. Rather than say the words it may be well for us to sit in silence and reverently listen in on Jesus' conversation with his Father.

1. Which phrase in the Our Father is most important for you today?

2. In what sense is the Lord's prayer intensely "dangerous?"

3. Do you pray the Our Father differently when alone than when you pray it with others?

Praying with the Church

　　Father,
　　look on us, your children.
　　Through the discipline of Lent

help us to grow in our desire for you.
We ask this through our Lord Jesus Christ, your Son,
who lives and reigns with You and the Holy Spirit,
one God, for ever and ever.

WEDNESDAY of the FIRST WEEK of LENT
Luke 11:29–32

I S IT POSSIBLE for a whole generation to go astray, to wander far from God's will? Often evil and wickedness are attributed to an individual who commits some heinous crime. But to label a generation as wicked is strong language. Lent is a time of examination, individual and collective; it is a time to pray for simplicity and for making our wandering ways straight once more.

Refrain: "This evil and faithless generation asks for a sign, but no sign will be given it except the sign of the prophet Jonah."

A WREATH

A wreathed garland of deserved praise,
Of praise deserved, unto thee I give,
I give to thee, who knowest all my ways,
My crooked winding ways, wherein I live,
Wherein I die, not live: for life is straight,
Straight as a line, and ever tends to thee,
To thee, who art more far above deceit,
Than deceit seems above simplicity.

Give me simplicity, that I may live,
So live and like, that I may know thy ways,
Know them and practice them: then shall I give
For this poor wreath, give thee a crown of praise.

George Herbert

God knows all our ways, all our motives, all our deepest desires. If
they are crooked, we are called to repentance; if straight, we offer
our God praise. We need desperately the graces of simplicity to
see what really gives life. Such simplicity enables us to make life-
giving choices.

But deceit infects us all. Everyone stands in need of salvation,
and Jesus came precisely to liberate us from sin and give us eternal
life. Insofar as we turn toward the light of grace our generation
will be healed. If we choose "crooked winding ways" our age will
end in death's darkness.

1. When do you offer God fitting praise?

2. How does one move from deceit to simplicity?

3. How does the path you presently tread compare to the way
   of Jesus?

Praying with the Church

Lord,
look upon us and hear our prayer.
By the good works you inspire,
help us to discipline our bodies
and to be renewed in spirit.
Grant this through our Lord Jesus Christ, your Son,
who lives and reigns with You and the Holy Spirit,
one God, for ever and ever.

THURSDAY of the FIRST WEEK of LENT
Matthew 7:7–12

L ENT is a good time to do inventories. What are the gifts God has given us? How well have we cultivated and shared the Lord's blessings? What do we still need to deepen our faith and become more mature disciples? Jesus invites us to approach God with confidence and trust.

Refrain: "If you, evil as you are, know how to give your children what is good, how much more will your Father in heaven pour out his gifts on all who pray to him."

THE PULLEY

When God at first made man,
Having a glass of blessings standing by;
Let us (said he) pour on him all we can:
Let the world's riches, which dispersed lie,
    Contract into a span.

So strength first made a way;
Then beauty flow'd, then wisdom, honor, pleasure:
When almost all was out, God made a stay,
Perceiving that alone of all his treasure
    Rest in the bottom lay.

For if I should (said he)
Bestow this jewel also on my creature,
He would adore my gifts instead of me,
And rest in Nature, not the God of Nature:
    So both should losers be.

Yet let him keep the rest,
But keep them with repining restlessness:

Let him be rich and weary, that at least,
If goodness lead him not, yet weariness
May toss him to my breast.

George Herbert

Our providential God pours out countless blessings upon creation. Taking nothing for granted is a challenge for everyone. Joyous thanksgiving is a goal of Christian living.

A distinction is necessary on our journey of faith, the distinction between the Giver and the gift. As a pilgrim people we never quite arrive at our destination. Thus we feel, in the depths of our being, a restlessness that disturbs our quietest days. God's pulley is the instrument by which we are drawn home. Lent reminds us that all finite gifts, good and honorable as they are, are less than God. Even the greatest blessing must be foregone if it blocks union with God.

1. Have you ever had the experience of a gift turning into an idol?

2. Have you ever asked for the gift of uncreated grace, for the gift of God as God?

3. What is being asked of you today? By God? By a co-worker? By your soul?

Praying with the Church

Father,
without you we can do nothing.
By your Spirit help us to know what is right
and to be eager in doing your will.
We ask this through our Lord Jesus Christ, your Son,
who lives and reigns with You and the Holy Spirit,
one God, for ever and ever.

FRIDAY of the FIRST WEEK of LENT
Matthew 5:20–26

T HE KINGDOM OF HEAVEN, the "place" where God reigns, is not experienced by those who injure and hate, by those who refuse reconciliation. Rather, since God is love, the kingdom is possessed by people who practice the virtue of love. This great power transforms our lives and the world. This virtue is a gift empowering us to bring the kingdom into history.

Refrain: "If your virtue does not surpass that of the Scribes and Pharisees, you will never enter into the kingdom of heaven."

LOVE (III)

Love bade me welcome: yet my soul drew back,
  Guilty of dust and sin.
But Quick-ey'd Love, observing me grow slack
  From my first entrance in,
Drew nearer to me, sweetly questioning,
  If I lack'd anything.

A guest, I answer'd, worthy to be here:
  Love said, You shall be he.
I the unkind, ungrateful? Ah my dear,
  I cannot look on thee.
Love took my hand, and smiling did reply,
  Who made the eyes but I?

Truth Lord, but I have marr'd them: let my shame
  Go where it doth deserve.
And know you not, says Love, who bore the blame?
  My dear, then I will serve.

> You must sit down, says Love, and taste my meat:
> So I did sit and eat.

George Herbert

Each day an invitation is sent our way. We are invited to enter into the presence of God and taste the abundance of divine love and mercy. God, this "quick-eyed" Lover, yearns for communion with the people formed in the divine image. God, always taking the initiative, continually reaches out into our lives, seeking to bring us to peace and fullness of life.

But we kill one another, hold grudges and resentments, refuse to extend the forgiveness given to us. In our honest moments we know we are not worthy to dwell in the presence of God because of our dust and sin, our ingratitude and unkindnesses. Our hope lies in the power of God whose light is stronger than our darkness, whose grace is mightier than our sin, whose life conquers all death.

1. Have you ever entered God's tent?

2. What does the refrain "Lord, I am not worthy to receive you, but only say the word and I shall be healed" mean to you?

3. Does Love lead to action (service) or to contemplation (sit and eat)?

Praying with the Church

Lord,
may our observance of Lent
help to renew us and prepare us
to celebrate the death and resurrection of Christ.

Grant this through our Lord Jesus Christ, your Son,
who lives and reigns with You and the Holy Spirit,
one God, for ever and ever.

SATURDAY of the FIRST WEEK of LENT
Matthew 5:43–48

H OLINESS is love come to perfection. Our constant prayer
might well be "Teach me thy love to know," a love that even
embraces those who hate and persecute us. Humanly speaking,
such a response is impossible; with grace, all things are possible.
We are invited into the perfection (the love) of God.

Refrain: "If you want to be true children of your heavenly Father,
then you must pray for those who persecute you and speak all
kinds of evil against you, says the Lord."

MATINS

I cannot ope mine eyes,
But thou art ready there to catch
My morning soul and sacrifice:
Then we must needs for that day make a match.

My God, what is a heart?
Silver, or gold, or precious stone,
Or star, or rainbow, or a part
Of all these things, or all of them in one?

My God, what is a heart,
That thou shouldst it so eye, and woo,
Pouring upon it all thy art,
As if that thou hadst nothing else to do?

Indeed man's whole estate
Amounts (and richly) to serve thee:
He did not heav'n and earth create,
Yet studies them, not him by whom they be.

Teach me thy love to know;
That this new light, which now I see,
May both the work and workman show:
Then by a sunbeam I will climb to thee.

George Herbert

What makes possible the love of friend and foe is the constant grace God offers to us. Every morning and every night the presence of God is at work transforming our hearts. The poet Francis Thompson was right in calling God "this tremendous lover."

A good Lenten prayer: "Teach me thy love to know." We might even add other infinitives — "to feel" and "to do." Full knowledge of God causes us to experience God's intimacy and to do God's will. The light of a new day with its illuminating love gives us life. All we have to do is find a sunbeam and climb home.

1. When was the last time you paused and took a serious look at a sunbeam?

2. How far does your love reach? the city limits? the county line? the galaxy?

3. Do you have an enemy (or two) who awaits your love and forgiveness?

Praying with the Church

Eternal Father,
turn our hearts to you.
By seeking your kingdom
and loving one another,
may we become a people who worship you
in spirit and truth
Grant this through our Lord Jesus Christ, your Son,
who lives and reigns with You and the Holy Spirit,
one God, for ever and ever.

SECOND WEEK OF LENT

SECOND SUNDAY of LENT

Matthew 17:1–9 (A); Mark 9:2–10 (B);
Luke 9:28–36 (C)

Mountains, a common biblical image, are sacred places: a place of prayer, a geography of the sacred, a circumstance that sets us apart from the busyness of daily life. Jesus spent time on mountains as well as in synagogues, communing with God and sharing faith experiences. Peter, James, and John were privileged to see Jesus in his glory. They would also be invited to share deeply in his suffering, the cross. Through baptism we too are given opportunities to encounter God in nature and human constructions, on mountains and in churches. We need only believe to know the mystery of transfiguration and personal transformation.

Refrain: "Our Lord Jesus Christ abolished death, and through the Gospel he revealed eternal life."

In Church

Often I try
To analyse the quality
Of its silences. Is this where God hides
From my searching? I have stopped to listen,

After the few people have gone,
To the air recomposing itself
For vigil. It has waited like this
Since the stones grouped themselves about it.
These are the hard ribs
Of a body that our prayers have failed
To animate. Shadows advance
From their corners to take possession
Of places the light held
For an hour. The bats resume
Their business. The uneasiness of the pews
Ceases. There is no other sound of a man
Breathing, testing his faith
On emptiness, nailing his questions
One by one to an untenanted cross.

R. S. Thomas

In Jesus, God is present and manifest. Our searching for a hidden God ends when Jesus reveals himself according to his exquisite timing. For our part, we need but be silent. God is here-now; it is we who are hiding from divine truth and mercy. As God looked for Adam in Eden, so God looks for us in the cool of the evening.

It is hard to keep vigil in the shadows and silences of the church, in the roughed terrain of the mountains. We become as uneasy as the pews longing for some activity to give us meaning. Soundlessness is fearful for it may reveal our poverty and total dependency upon the Lord. It is good for us to be in the dark, regardless of the pain. Faith is all that is required — and some love.

On the mountain and in our churches we come to a tenanted cross. Jesus was crucified for our sins; Jesus died to bring us salvation. Here is the glory that makes life radiant. It is the glory of love incarnate and a love given unto death. Nothing less than the cross could convince us of God's salvific and extravagant love.

1. How does emptiness test your faith?
2. How does God reveal himself to you?
3. Why is the cross the glory of God?

Praying with the Church

God our Father,
help us to hear your Son.
Enlighten us with your word
that we may find the way to your glory.
We ask this through our Lord Jesus Christ, your Son,
who lives and reigns with you and the Holy Spirit,
one God, for ever and ever.

MONDAY of the SECOND WEEK of LENT
Luke 6:36–38

A NOVELIST once claimed that there is only one tragedy in life — not to be a saint. We become holy by imitating God's compassion and forgiveness, by participating in God's love and concern, by following Jesus in a life of obedience and self-giving. In the end, saints look more like twisted steel than shining gold.

Refrain: "Be compassionate and forgiving as your Father is, says the Lord."

A SAINT

We look for mystic gold
And silvered ecstasy
and find a tempered, twisted piece
of steel.

Gordon Gilsdorf

Have you seen a saint lately? And where do you look to find one?
Perhaps we head for the church or a temple, hoping to catch a
glimpse of God's agent. Or we may go to the cloister in search
of an ascetical mystic. Then again our looking may take us to
the kitchen table, the factory, the board room, where we discover
kindness and love in action.

Saints seldom reflect gold. Rather they are steely people who
have been tempered by temptation, twisted into wholeness by the
crosses of life. Look at the mother of Jesus, tested by the sword
and suffering. Look at the great St. Paul, broken and healed by
a gracious savior. Mystic gold is illusory; tempered, twisted steel,
authentic strength.

1. Have you met a saint this past week?

2. What does holiness mean for you? Is the "perfection of
   charity" a good description?

3. Who is your favorite saint? When was the last time you
   two talked?

Praying with the Church

God our Father,
teach us to find new life through penance.
Keep us from sin,
and help us to live by your commandment of love.

We ask this through our Lord Jesus Christ, your Son,
who lives and reigns with You and the Holy Spirit,
one God, for ever and ever.

TUESDAY of the SECOND WEEK of LENT
Matthew 23:1–12

TEACHING is one thing; practicing what is taught is another.
Jesus not only instructed us in the meaning of love but lived
it. When all is said and done, Jesus had but "one" word in his
vocabulary. The Scribes and Pharisees had hundreds if not thousands. Jesus lived his word; the Scribes and Pharisees failed to
put the truth into action.

Refrain: "You have one *teacher*, and he is in heaven. *Christ* your
Lord."

LYRICS FOR THE CHRISTIAN

1. To Christ

You are my lantern for night,
   slowly tunneling this dark,
bartering one world of light
for another, and blinding fright.
The dank air you landmark
   with meaning, warmth and sight.

2. Following Christ

This way is lightly traveled. The moss
    Is hardly worn from stone.
Yet pilgrims in the shadow of the cross
    Will never walk alone.

3. Cross Reference

I searched
God's lexicon
To fathom "Bethlehem"
And "Calvary." It simply said:
See "Love."

Gordon Gilsdorf

The divine dictionary is surprisingly small. We are reminded by St. John the Evangelist that "God is love." Thus when we attempt to fathom the meaning of the birth, ministry, and death of Jesus, we have a central referential point: divine love.

Lent is a season for deepening our life in Christ. We are invited to appropriate his words, his attitudes, his manner of dealing with others. In our attempt to nurture Christian living we consistently return to the commandment of love of God and neighbor. This involves respect, reverence, active concern, and compassion.

1. What are the ten most important words in your vocabulary?

2. Besides Bethlehem and Calvary, what other sites in the life of Jesus are explained by love? Cana? Jordan? Gethsemane?

3. How does Jesus instruct you in the ways of love?

Praying with the Church

Lord,
watch over your Church,
and guide it with your unfailing love.
Protect us from what could harm us
and lead us to what will save us.
Help us always,
for without you we are bound to fail.
Grant this through our Lord Jesus Christ, your Son
who lives and reigns with You and the Holy Spirit,
one God, for ever and ever.

WEDNESDAY of the SECOND WEEK of LENT
Matthew 20:17–28

T WO INVITATIONS come our way: an invitation to union and to service. Jesus is always inviting individuals, James and John, Zacchaeus and Paul, you and me, to dwell in his presence and then go forth to share the gifts received. It's not places of honor nor prestige for which we were called and invited. Rather, to receive and share God's love.

Refrain: "The Son of Man did not come to be served but to serve, and to give his life as a ransom for many."

INVITATION

After childhood
no one climbs a tree
but a thief,
Zacchaeus or Dismas:
soon or late
the invitation,
"Climb down,
come home!"

Gordon Gilsdorf

When was the last time you climbed a tree, the last time you took a serious risk in pursuing what is deepest within you? Zacchaeus climbed a sycamore tree to see Jesus; a thief, from the tree of the cross, was at eye level with the Lord; Dismas too encountered God by divine grace. Each of them heard the call to return to their true self and fulfill their vocation.

The universal call and vocation of us all is a call to holiness, the perfection of charity. Our lives are to be lives of service, like the life of Jesus. To fulfill that calling we need to experience the Spirit who enlightens, enkindles, and enables us to discern and do God's will.

1. Whom are you being asked to serve today?

2. How has Jesus ransomed your life?

3. In what way does Jesus invite you into his presence? What does he then commission you to do?

Praying with the Church

Father,
teach us to live good lives,

encourage us with your support
and bring us to eternal life.
We ask this through our Lord Jesus Christ, your Son,
who lives and reigns with You and the Holy Spirit,
one God, for ever and ever.

THURSDAY of the SECOND WEEK of LENT
Luke 16:19–31

L IFE is a journey filled with hills, crossroads, and some mighty dark woods. Some travel in luxury, fine linen, colorful dress, rich tables. Others, like Lazarus and thousands of street people, have little consolation along the way. The poet R. S. Thomas once asked: "Are not our lives harbours?" The Lenten answer is a resounding yes.

Refrain: "Son, remember the good things you received in your lifetime and the bad things Lazarus received in his."

How WEARY THE ROAD

How weary the road
in sunlight
without a shady wood
to cool the day!

How poor the pilgrim
without the needy

> to care for
> along the way!
>
> How dull the travel
> without a hill
> to climb or crossroad
> to lead astray!
>
> How tiring the journey
> without a rest
> at nightfall,
> without a place to stay!
>
> *Gordon Gilsdorf*

One identity of the church is that of the pilgrim people. On the pilgrimage we are challenged to care for the needy, provide shelter for the homeless, offer rest to the weary. Jesus models for us the life of the servant, the pilgrim who was for and with others.

When God sends the Holy Spirit into our lives, making strong our faith and hope, then we become active in the works of love. The road is no longer weary but filled with high adventure leading to the kingdom. Without God's Spirit, fatigue and cynicism dominate our lives.

1. Who are the needy people God has placed in your path this week?

2. What hills has the Lord asked you to climb, the crossroads demanding a decision?

3. Why are fine linen, rich foods, expensive garments so dangerous?

Praying with the Church
   God of love,
   bring us back to you.

Send your Spirit to make us strong in faith
and active in good works.
Grant this through our Lord Jesus Christ, your Son,
who lives and reigns with You and the Holy Spirit,
one God, for ever and ever.

FRIDAY of the SECOND WEEK of LENT
Matthew 21:33–43, 45–46

G OODNESS AND EVIL! The battles rage down through the
centuries good seeds and bad seeds! Within each of us
we must be ready to discern the light from the darkness. Jesus
tells us stories that we might see ourselves as we are. The truth
sometimes hurts.

Refrain: "He will bring those evil men to an end and entrust his
vineyard to other tenants who will give him the harvest at the
proper season."

THE WONDER OF GOOD

Goodness flowers our dismal years
like springtime's need to surpass
itself with a clutch of root
and the reach of color and class.

And goodness heaps our dying world
like autumn's feverish gathering:

all that summers in field and flock
winter buries for another spring.

The wonder of good, then, like evil,
is its slow unfolding until we die.
Perhaps that is the bloom we hear
when we go to God, forever in His eye.

Gordon Gilsdorf

Given the violence and injustice of our times, it is difficult to appreciate the goodness that surrounds us. Some even question whether we have lost our capacity to wonder, to contemplate God's creative work. Faith is the needed grace in times of blindness.

Goodness does flower, producing the harvest we call the kingdom. Truth replaces the lie, charity overcomes indifference, freedom unties the bonds of enslavement, justice removes oppression and fear. Goodness is slowly unfolding and in the end will conquer evil and death.

1. What can you do today to add to the pool of goodness?

2. What vineyard (gifts) has the Lord entrusted to you?

3. When we go to God, what words would you like to hear?

Praying with the Church

Merciful Father,
may our acts of penance bring us your forgiveness.
Open our hearts to your love,
and prepare us for the coming feast of the resurrection.
We ask this through our Lord Jesus Christ, your Son,
who lives and reigns with You and the Holy Spirit,
one God, for ever and ever.

SATURDAY of the SECOND WEEK of LENT
Luke 15:1–3, 11–32

T HE PRODIGAL son and his elder brother are well-known biblical characters. One wasted much of his life; the other suffered from self-righteousness and resentment. Both reveal aspects of our own character and help us to enter into deeper conversion. And the main celebrity, the prodigal father, reveals to us the extravagance of God's gracious mercy.

Refrain: "Father, I have sinned against heaven and against you; I no longer deserve to be called your son; treat me as one of your servants."

GOSPEL CELEBRITIES

1
The way Peter said
   "We have left everything," you'd
      think he owned a fleet.

2
Nicodemus, thanks
   for asking that dumb question
      for the rest of us.

3
Five loaves and two fish
   out of hand, a boy sees them
      shared beyond his dreams.

4
The tree of Eden,
   was it a sycamore tree
      like yours, Zacchaeus?

5
Never one to waste
    a gathering, Naim's widow
        gave them a party.

6
Who is Himself bread,
    Whose word Mary takes as bread,
        still needs Martha's bread.

7
Did the Easter news
    make you pause at each new door,
        afraid, Barabbas?

Gordon Gilsdorf

And the list goes on. I would add:

8
What did the pigs teach you,
    in that land of illusions,
        younger, now wiser son?

9
Elder and longer loved,
    resentment no way
        to come to a party.

10
A prodigal father,
    extravagant in joy and mercy,
        sounds like heaven.

1. With whom do you identify in this Gospel passage?

2. How do you link mercy and justice?

3. What are the details around your "I have sinned" statement?

Praying with the Church

God our Father,
by your gifts to us on earth
we already share in your life.
In all we do,
guide us to the light of your kingdom.
Grant this through our Lord Jesus Christ, your Son,
who lives and reigns with You and the Holy Spirit,
one God, for ever and ever.

THIRD WEEK OF LENT

᭶

THIRD SUNDAY of LENT
John 4:5–42 (A); John 2:13–25 (B);
Luke 13:1–9 (C)

DID JESUS write letters home to his mother and friends? No
report of this activity in the Gospel. And if he did, what
would have been the topics? Probably something about his encounter with a Samaritan woman at the well, or the time he went
to the temple and discovered his anger, or about the fig tree that
failed in its mission of life. So many things to share, so many
experiences of joy and sorrow. Whatever the topics, the letters
would have had some reference to his mission: doing the work of
his Father. Lent is good season to send and receive letters.

Refrain: "Destroy this temple, says the Lord, and in three days I
will rebuild it. He was speaking of the temple of this body."

THE LETTER

And to be able to put at the end
Of the letter Athens, Florence — some name
That the spirit recalls from earlier journeys

Through the dark wood, seeking the path
To the bright mansions; cities and towns
Where the soul added depth to its stature.

And not to worry about the date,
The words being timeless, concerned with truth,
Beauty, love, misery even,
Which has its seasons in the long growth
From seed to flesh, flesh to spirit.

And laying aside the pen, dipped
Not in tears' volatile liquid
But in black ink of the heart's well,
To read again what the hand has written
To the many voices' quiet dictation.

R. S. Thomas

At the end of the letter — to put Jericho, Jordan, Jerusalem. Cities and rivers and towns that made the soul deep with meaning. Sacred places these, sites of light and darkness. Despite the differences, something's always the same — the search to love and be loved.

Since words have something of eternity about them, the posted date is not significant. Timeless, the experiences of truth and beauty, love and misery. These are not governed by hours or minutes; these defy both our spatial and temporal categories. Heaven and earth merge in the sacrament of the heart.

When the pen is set aside, the letter folded and posted, we can review in our minds the message sent from the heart. It is a message of hope, of joy and sorrow, of struggle and success. The letter is about life lived in the mystery of God.

1. When was the last time you sent or received a "keeper" letter?

2. Why is letter writing a spiritual exercise?

3. If you wrote a Lenten letter to the Lord, what would you say?

Praying with the Church

Father,
you have taught us to overcome our sins
by prayer, fasting, and works of mercy.
When we are discouraged by our weakness,
give us confidence in your love.
We ask this through our Lord Jesus Christ, your Son,
who lives and reigns with you and the Holy Spirit,
one God, for ever and ever.

MONDAY of the THIRD WEEK of LENT
Luke 4:24–30

G OD ACTS in a variety of ways. Not infrequently, prophets are sent to remind us about who we are and where we are going. Quite often they are rejected because the message given is challenging or too threatening. And when God sends a prophet to his own country — trouble! Ask Elijah or Naaman. Ask the greatest of all prophets, Jesus. Yet come what may, the truth will have its day. Faithful prophets are willing to pay the price so that people can once again experience the acts of God.

Refrain: "I tell you assuredly no prophet is accepted in his own country."

ACTS OF GOD

"Immediate are the Acts of God" (John Milton)

Some say the Deity is distant,
only sending angels on divine errands,
now and then a child or a dove.
Others say God acts directly,
reversing mediation by immediate deeds.
No Church or sacraments needed
when direct transmission precludes intermediaries.

But back to the some — some say
immediate acts of God contain too much glory,
blinding the eye with excessive light,
deafening the ear with unmodified truth.
So God accommodates,
sensitive to our frail senses,
attuned to our fragile hearts.

Perhaps God's mediated acts alone
have immediate access to our souls.

Robert F. Morneau

Nature and history are two avenues of grace. God's manifestation
can be discovered by those possessing wonder and the eye of love.
Faith enables us to see the finger of God in doves and donuts,
in autumn and pain, in dreams and shattered promises. God is
active — and faithful.

God also enters our hearts through prophetic speech. Prophets
are born to tell the truth, whatever the price. Grace mediated

through words (and through the Word) is a given in our Christian tradition. We need but put our ear to the ground to again feel the footfall of our Savior.

1. How does God intervene in your life?

2. List five acts of God that you experienced yesterday.

3. What was your response to this activity? Praise? Thanksgiving? Fear? Wonder?

Praying with the Church
God of Mercy,
free your church from sin,
and protect it from evil.
Guide us, for we cannot be saved without you.
We ask this through our Lord Jesus Christ, your Son,
who lives and reigns with You and the Holy Spirit,
one God, for ever and ever.

TUESDAY of the THIRD WEEK of LENT
Matthew 18:21–35

ONE OF THE CHALLENGES of life is to remember. Spiritual Alzheimer's is a disease that can destroy our souls. Remember what? That God has forgiven us, extended divine mercy time and time again. How dare we then withhold this gift from others! Peter forgot he was forgiven and thus would impose limits on his own mercy. There is an antidote to spiritual Alzheimer's, the daily expression of God's mercy in Jesus.

Refrain: "The Lord said: Peter, I do not tell you to forgive only seven times, but seventy times seven."

SIN

"Trying to find the beginnings of sin is like..."
(Bernard MacLaverty)

A tangled ball of yarn was once ordered,
each strand in its proper place.
Then something happened.
Was it the wind working its havoc,
or a mischievous cat set upon chaos,
or a small child irresistibly attracted to color?
If the cause is in doubt, the effect is not.
Sheer mess.

And the entanglements of our lives?
The broken "web of exchange,"
the constant "missing the mark,"
the simple, devastating "disobedience"?
The fact is sin
whatever the ambiguous beginnings may have been.

Robert F. Morneau

We are concerned not only about the number of our sins but also the kinds of sins to be forgiven. Disobedience is quite obvious: told to love, we hate (Kyrie eleison); given an ideal, respect for all, we miss the mark and hold only our own in reverence (Christe eleison); called to live in oneness and peace we break the web of relationships and incur guilt and shame (Kyrie eleison).

The Lord continually breaks into our lives to repair our fences, untangle our messy minds, free us from our enslavements. We need a savior — one of the great lessons of Lent. We need mercy and we need to extend that same grace to those who enslave us and cause us injury.

1. How many times have you been forgiven since Ash Wednesday?

2. How do you describe sin: disobedience, missing the mark, breaking the "web of exchange"?

3. Do you know where your major sin begins?

Praying with the Church
Lord,
you call us to service,
and continue your saving work among us.
May your love never abandon us.
We ask this through our Lord Jesus Christ, your Son,
who lives and reigns with You and the Holy Spirit,
one God, for ever and ever.

WEDNESDAY of the THIRD WEEK of LENT
Matthew 5:17–19

ABOLISHING and fulfilling, two human activities. Lincoln helped to abolish slavery through his Emancipation Proclamation. Gandhi assisted in fulfilling India's dream for independence through his doctrine of non-violence. Jesus came to fulfill the law and the prophets; he came to abolish the darkness of sin and death. And why are we here? Lent gives us pause to reflect on this question.

Refrain: "The Lord said: do not think that I have come to abolish the law and the prophets; I have come not to abolish but to fulfill them."

GOD'S PRESENCE

It is there that God works,
the back side of the tapestry,
the underside of life:
in dark alleys of fear and doubt,
on the margins of poverty and pain,
at the muddled crossroads of heartache.
Don't look for the Deity elsewhere,
at galas or balls or luxurious banquets.
The Divine dwells only at one address:
"Love's Lane."

Robert F. Morneau

God can be found in the law and the prophets. Moses transmits guidelines and commandments for serious living. Isaiah informs us of God's calling us by name and holding us precious in his sight. Jesus fulfills the law and prophets by his life, death, and resurrection.

But God is found elsewhere as well. Jesus invites us to dine at the table of sinners, to seek out and save the stray, to embrace the orphan and widow. Since God is love we must look for the Deity in the land of charity.

1. How do you fulfill the law and the prophets?

2. Where do you look for God? Where does God look for you?

3. Who are the greatest and least in the kingdom of heaven?

Praying with the Church

> Lord,
> during this Lenten Season,
> nourish with your own word of life,
> and make us one in love and prayer.
> Grant this through our Lord Jesus Christ, your Son,
> who lives and reigns with You and the Holy Spirit,
> one God, for ever and ever.

THURSDAY of the THIRD WEEK of LENT
Luke 11:14–23

PREPOSITIONS are determinative. Being for or against God shapes our destiny. Faith reveals to us a passionate God who is with us in faithful, divine creativity, who is for us in the eucharistic body and blood of Christ, who is in us through the transformative power of the Spirit. Prepositions give us a Trinitarian spirituality at once passionate and challenging. That passion translates into healing us of our sin.

Refrain: "If it is by the power of God that I cast out devils, says the Lord, then the kingdom of heaven has come to you already."

A PASSIONATE GOD

"Is God filled with passion?"
Who is the God of Abraham of Ur,
 of St. Francis of Assisi,
 of Nikos Kazantzakis?

Have we, a generation of small believers,
 domesticated the Deity,
 draining the blush from the Creator's cheeks,
 defrocking Jesus of his bitter tears,
 imprisoning the Spirit who would soar and rent the sky?

Is God passionate?
 Volcanic in anger,
 oceanic in longing,
 abyssless in love,
 torrential in mercy?

Can God be otherwise
 or else
  or different from the Nazarene?

Robert F. Morneau

God's power flows out of love. At times that love appears as anger when our sinfulness is broken. At other times it is characterized by yearning as God draws us toward the kingdom. Again it appears as mercy as our guilt is peeled away. Whatever the experience, it is a divine passion that comes our way.

Jesus reveals God's passionate love. The dumb man spoke, the lame walked, the blind saw. That love reached out to the marginal and oppressed. That love is grounded in faith that hopefully awakens our compassion and fills us with faith.

1. Do you experience God as passionate?

2. What is the relationship between compassion and passion?

3. What prepositions define your life?

Praying with the Church

Father,
help us to be ready to celebrate the great paschal mystery.
Make our love grow each day,
as we approach the feast of our salvation.
We ask this through our Lord Jesus Christ, your Son,
who lives and reigns with You and the Holy Spirit,
one God, for ever and ever.

FRIDAY of the THIRD WEEK of LENT
Mark 12:28–34

ANSWERING LARGE QUESTIONS is not all that difficult. The trouble comes in living the answers — "walking the talk." The greatest commandment? Even a third grader exposed to a catechism might hit upon the answer of love. Our Lenten challenge is to take the answer and translate it into action. Lent is a time of incarnation.

Refrain: "Teacher, what is the greatest commandment in the law? Jesus said to him: you shall love the Lord your God with your whole heart."

Consumed by Love

"Anything less than God is just a messenger."
(Wm. Johnston)

I like things less than God:
    the taste of apple cider in early fall;
    the smell of newly mown hay at dawn;
    the sound of the oboe's ancient melancholy;
    the sight of a circling hawk against the blue sky.

But I also like things "more than" God:
    fire — the source of every star;
    water — so vast no ocean can hold;
    air — reaching out to infinity;
    earth — solid, grounded in immensity.

All messengers are, in the end, inarticulate,
the message too large for words,
the mystery too vast for fingers to hold.

But were God to come, undisguised,
we would vanish, consumed by Love.

Robert F. Morneau

Love is not only a commandment but a great mystery. In some way love brings about oneness that overflows into peace and joy. In commanding us to love, God wants to make his peace felt in time and space. We mediate that presence with varying degrees of success and failure.

If God were to bypass apple cider, new mown hay, the stars and sea, we would be blinded and overwhelmed. Yet we are one day destined to be consumed by love; we are destined to meet God face to face. Lent moves us a few inches closer to that oneness.

1. How did you mediate God's love yesterday?

2. Are letters sometimes better than personal encounters?

3. Which messages best reveal to you the mystery of God?

Praying with the Church

Merciful Father,
fill our hearts with your love,
and keep us faithful to the Gospel of Christ.
Grant us the grace to rise above our human weakness.
Grant this through our Lord Jesus Christ, your Son,
who lives and reigns with You and the Holy Spirit,
one God, for ever and ever.

⚜

SATURDAY of the THIRD WEEK of LENT
Luke 18:9–14

WE ALL GENUFLECT to someone, something. It may be our own ego, or money, or power, or prestige, or the God who made and sustains us. Humility places us in the arena of truth urging us to kneel and strike our breasts. Arrogance blinds us to our true human condition and distances us from God's loving touch. Lenten humility is a gift to pray for.

Refrain: "The tax collector stood far away and would not raise his eyes to heaven. He struck his breast and prayed: God, have mercy on me, a sinner."

SALVATION

"Between the stirrup and the ground / He salvation found"
(Anon.)

A free fall seems hardly liberating,
more like a topsy tumble called precariousness.
Yet when the horse called life bucks,
the rider sent airborne on his way to solid earth,
we ponder what might be found in the fall.

Adam lost salvation in the toss of an apple core,
Eve and the serpent rode bareback
on the wild stallion east of Eden.
Where now to experience the Messiah? From whence, salvation?

Between the stirrup and the ground, fear dwells.
It ignites the fire of wisdom,
which enkindles the cry for help.
Salvation is found not on the ground
but in mid-air — in the poverty of helplessness.

Even the wild stallion turns to see the miracle,
a thrown rider whose fall is victorious.

Robert F. Morneau

Finding salvation is a Lenten goal. Some find it in the temple, others in being tossed to the ground, most in the land of humility. Salvation can also be lost by a mind-set that denies our helplessness and our personal sin.

God, in amazing paradoxes, saves us by imprisoning us in his love. By dying we find life, by falling we rise, by failing we gain our victory. All is turned upside down by the Gospel.

1. What do you genuflect to?

2. Where do you find salvation and hope?

3. On a scale of 1 to 10 what is your degree of humility / arrogance?

Praying with the Church

Lord,
make this Lenten observance,
know the suffering, death, and resurrection of Christ.
Bring us to the full joy of Easter.
We ask this through our Lord Jesus Christ, your Son,
who lives and reigns with You and the Holy Spirit,
one God, for ever and ever.

FOURTH WEEK OF LENT

FOURTH SUNDAY of LENT
John 9:1–41 (A); John 3:14–21 (B);
Luke 15:1–3, 11–32 (C)

THE SCRIPTURES tell us of God's great love for the world, a love that cures a blind man, a love that embraces the prodigal son, a love that transforms lives and makes them whole. When that love is made manifest and is experienced deeply, we then have some awareness of God's kingdom, a kingdom of truth, love, freedom, and justice. During these Lenten days we continue to pray, asking God to make the kingdom of peace come into the world. That kingdom seems far off but is truly near, as near as the breath of God's abiding love.

Refrain: "It was unheard of for anyone to open the eyes of a man born blind until the coming of Christ, the son of God."

THE KINGDOM

It's a long way off but inside it
There are quite different things going on.
Festivals at which the poor man
Is king and the consumptive is

Healed; mirrors in which the blind look
At themselves and love looks at them
Back; and industry is for mending
The bent bones and the minds fractured
By life. It's a long way off, but to get
There takes no time and admission
Is free, if you will purge yourself
Of desire, and present yourself with
Your need only and the simple offering
Of your faith, green as a leaf.

R. S. Thomas

Inside the kingdom are many surprises. At the head table are the poor and the least, offered rich foods, choicest wines, loving conversation. In the kingdom the blind see and are seen by Love. Now all work and human activity contains reverence for life and war is no more.

Though the kingdom may seem distant, such is not the case. It's close, real close. And yet another surprise — no charge exacted except a loving, forgiving, faith-filled heart. Time and space, the chancellors of our human condition, no longer limit us. Eternity knocks down all barriers to communion.

Yet the kingdom does have a requirement: faith. It may be a young, immature faith ("green as a leaf"). It may be the faith of Abraham, ancient and firm. Whatever, this faith involves trust in God's saving help, assent to God's gracious word, obedience to the Lordship of Jesus Christ. This "simple" offering positions us at the threshold of the kingdom.

1. What does your Lenten faith look like?

2. How did you experience God's kingdom this past week?

3. What desire is God asking you to purge out of your heart?

Praying with the Church

Father of peace,
we are joyful in your Word,
your Son Jesus Christ,
who reconciles us to you.
Let us hasten toward Easter
with the eagerness of faith and love.
We ask this through our Lord Jesus Christ, your Son,
who lives and reigns with you and the Holy Spirit,
one God, for ever and ever.

MONDAY of the FOURTH WEEK of LENT
John 4:43–54

JESUS MAKES VISIBLE the compassion of God. His heart is deeply moved by the suffering of a child, the anguish of a parent, the despair of a sinner. Baptized into his life, we too are to walk the paths that lead to those in pain. We too must be open to the cry of the poor.

Refrain: "A royal official, hearing that Jesus had come to Galilee, begged him to heal his son who lay ill in Capernaum."

MOTHER TERESA

When Mother Teresa holds a child,
she holds a star.
"See what I have plucked from the rubble
there on back the stairs where rats were nibbling."

She holds it close as though
this were the one living light
and she must warm her fingers in its beauty.
"See what I have plucked from the pavement,
a star fallen from God's crown.
Do you think, my brothers, my sisters,
that there can be too many stars,
too many lights on the earth?"

Brother Edward Seifert, F.S.C.

The work of Jesus continues in our times. God sends forth individuals and communities to make present and manifest divine concern. Whether in the streets of Calcutta or Chicago, the mountains of Peru or the Ukraine, the deserts of North Africa or Arizona, angels of mercy come to heal the fallen stars, the bruised reeds, the wavering flames.

The danger of being overwhelmed by numbers and the sheer volume of suffering is real. Our temptation is to yield to compassion fatigue, to view the magnitude of needs and be discouraged to even begin. Yet the call comes singularly — go now to Capernaum or Los Angeles or Jakarta. One star, one light at a time. No more, no less, is asked of each of us.

1. Whom have you plucked from the rubbles of life?

2. Where do you find Jesus working today in our world?

3. What beauty do those in dire need offer to us?

Praying with the Church

Father, Creator,
you give the world new life by your sacraments.
May we, your Church, grow in your life
and continue to receive your help on earth.

Grant this through our Lord Jesus Christ, your Son,
who lives and reigns with You and the Holy Spirit,
one God, for ever and ever.

TUESDAY of the FOURTH WEEK of LENT
John 5:1–16

WELLNESS is an "in" word. Programs of discipline and rigorous routine are established to assist people as they strive to get in shape. Jesus was concerned with "wellness": "Do you want to get well again?" is the question addressed to a man who was ill for thirty-eight years. What joy to witness the wounded man picking up his mat and walking! What a miracle of faith!

Refrain: "The man who cured me told me to pick up my sleeping mat and go in peace."

THE TASSEL OF HIS CLOAK

All that I wanted that day was to follow the voice
of him who was drawing me closer
through the mutter and mumble
and clack of the crowd that was milling around him.
The pain in my side I bore bravely,
the pain that kept pulsing
at each step that I took.
I saw a break in the throng

that surged him. I caught sight of his cloak
and, sparked by new hope, I reached for the tassel and
    touched it.
I shook with joy as I touched it.
He stopped and his eyes started searching.
He at once found me.
"Someone has touched me," he told the people around him.
I went down on my knees and cried out my need.
He came near and lifted me to him, saying,
slowly and gently, "Daughter, your faith has healed you."
I stood up with delight and groped for support.
I stood free of my pain.
I stood there and loved him forever.

Brother Edward Seifert, F.S.C.

Like the man in today's Gospel, the woman of this poem encounters Jesus. Everything is changed. A new freedom is won far
beyond the disappearance of pain, a freedom that empowers love.
The very presence of Jesus is salvific. One needs but a modicum
of faith, a slight touch of his tassel, the fall of his shadow, and
all will be well.

Our lives are also in need of emancipation. Like the long-
suffering man on the mat, like the woman bent over with pain,
we too need to be liberated from whatever evils lurk in our hearts
or relationships. Jesus desires life, life in abundance. His presence
can still be felt in word and sacrament if we have but faith.

1. What pains continue to reoccur in your life?

2. Where can you go to touch, be touched by Jesus?

3. What is the relationship between freedom and love?

Praying with the Church

Father,
may our Lenten observance
prepare us to embrace the paschal mystery
and to proclaim your salvation with joyful praise.
We ask this through our Lord Jesus Christ, your Son,
who lives and reigns with You and the Holy Spirit,
one God, for ever and ever.

WEDNESDAY of the FOURTH WEEK of LENT
John 5:17–30

S OME THINGS are a matter of life or death, food being one example, air another. But the soul also needs to be sustained, and Jesus tells us that his words, listened to and appropriated, lead to eternal life. The reverse is also true: not to be nourished by God's thoughts and life is to experience the deepest of deaths. Jesus is clear about his mission: the doing of his Father's will. That will is that life might be experienced to the full so much so that even death becomes a divine instrument in the achievement of salvation.

Refrain: "Whoever hears my word, says the Lord, and believes in him who sent me, has eternal life."

DEATH, LUMINOUS DEATH
(To the memory of Brothers Alphansus & Vincent)

Let death, luminous death,
let death divest the darkness
and let the light shine forth
so that we can see more clearly the aging dancers
performing there against mercy's backdrops,
dancers who show their grace
in bending and stooping and raising other men upward.
They are God's dancers who show their powers
with pointer and chalk and design,
with lens and light and screen
as they lift men upward to see
figures of unknown Godhead.

The dancers have fallen,
and the God who has loved them has raised them
to dance after death,
where walls without end mirror their perfect bodies.
They leap and they lunge
they pause and sweep on, those perfect bodies,
and it seems they are beckoning us upward
to them, to luminous death,
and to dance after death and the darkness.

Brother Edward Seifert, F.S.C.

Death hardly seems luminous to our age. On the contrary, it is the darkest night instilling fear and anxiety. The finite human mind, distanced from faith, falters before the fatalism of mortality. The dance is over, the heartbeats stop. Time yields not to eternity but to nothingness.

Jesus comes to do the will of God. The will is eternal, full life, a dance after darkness and death. The dead will leave their graves, the dead will hear the Son's voice, the dead will pass into the fullness of life. As one of the church's ancient hymns proclaims: "In death the dawn of perfect day."

1. What is your attitude toward death?

2. When was the last time you took a silent walk through a cemetery?

3. Was C. S. Lewis correct in saying that this life is a "Shadowland" and that "death exposes us into full reality?"

Praying with the Church

Lord,
you reward virtue
and forgive the repentant sinner.
Grant us your forgiveness
as we come before you confessing our guilt.
We ask this through our Lord Jesus Christ, your Son,
who lives and reigns with You and the Holy Spirit,
one God, for ever and ever.

THURSDAY of the FOURTH WEEK of LENT
John 5:31–47

TRUTH IS ROUGH. We dare not romanticize it or we may well have a rude awakening. John the Baptist testified to the truth in prophetic tones that shocked the crowds. But Jesus' testimony is greater still as we watch his healing power and the compassionate forgiveness of sin. Nor was any of this for human approval. Rather, it was all done for God's glory, all done that the truth of God's love might set us free.

Refrain: "Jesus bore testimony to the truth, and although I have no need of human testimony, says the Lord, I remind you of this for your own salvation."

GOD IS NOT NICE

God is not nice.
Frankly I would think twice
before inviting him to tea.
He would bore us with long silences
and sit and crumble cake
and eye us owlishly.

I am sure I would be hard pressed
before I would make a house guest
of this king. He would untidy
my chaste rooms with sudden
gusts of grandeur, and I would be picking up
all day after the Almighty.

In truth I would become delirious
living with this imperious
Lover. He would rip the fine design
I have stitched for my pleasant days,
saying, "I must be rude
if I am to be divine."

Brother Edward Seifert, F.S.C.

The psalmist tells us that God is compassionate and kind. The poet testifies to another attribute of God: rudeness. Is this some loose, heretical poetic license or a metaphor of disturbing truth? Does God rip apart our self-centered designs that we might begin to live full human lives?

Both the psalmist and the poet would agree on one thing: that God is an imperious Lover. Jesus testifies to this by his works. Divine love is extravagant and excludes no one. With gusts of grandeur and judgment, our souls are cleansed of sin and sadness so that our rooms might become fit dwelling places for the divine guest.

1. When was the last time you had God over for tea?

2. Is rudeness a necessary quality of divinity?

3. Are you comfortable in the silence of God?

Praying with the Church

Merciful Father,
may the presence of our Lenten observance
make us your obedient people.
May the love within us be seen in what we do
and lead us to the joy of Easter.
Grant this through our Lord Jesus Christ, your Son,
who lives and reigns with You and the Holy Spirit,
one God, for ever and ever.

FRIDAY of the FOURTH WEEK of LENT
John 7:1–2, 10, 25–30

J ESUS, THE MESSIAH, was a hunted man. A threat to those
in power, he became the object of their violence. Yet he was
not deterred from going to Jerusalem to continue his mission of
salvation. Though the people missed his true ancestry, Jesus knew
that his life was grounded in the Father and that his task was to
seek out and save the lost. The work of the Messiah was dirty
business demanding total self-giving.

Refrain: "Indeed you know me, says the Lord, and you know
where I come from. Yet I have not come of my own accord; it
was my Father who sent me."

HE SPOKE OF CHRIST

He spoke and the Christ he showed
as we leaned to see him was not
the graceful treader of meadows, the breather
of honeyed secrets to cloistered maidens,
but a man with dust and sweat on his face,
unwashed feet and eyes too tired for weeping.
We heard and we knew this Christ, for we
had met. Together we had scraped
and scrabbled on the rocks.
We had in our dim rooms together groped
to ease with words the long-shared sadness.

He spoke and the Lord we turned to
had no nine promises of comfort, no
cool transepts for his own. His hair
hung uncared for and unfragrant.
His eyes burned with seeing

what was in man.
Better than cloistered girl at mystic prayer
we saw him in infrangible embrace
of foul and bleeding, spent, black-wounded man.

Brother Edward Seifert, F.S.C.

One way to figure out where a person comes from is to study what direction that person is going. Jesus came from a God of love and went where that love could be made visible: in the lives of the hurting and needy, in the hearts of the lonely and despairing, in the home of sinners and saints. Holy cards seldom give us clues to the real Jesus: bleeding hands and bruised feet will.

When Jesus emptied himself of divinity, he took on our human condition: dust and tears, sweat and strain, headaches and heartaches, ecstasy and joy. Our road became his path; our exile, his home. Wherever we find the poor and persecuted, we will find Christ. From the outside, not a pretty picture, but within, sheer radiance.

1. When you speak of Christ, what is your message?

2. Has your image of Christ changed this Lent?

3. What promises (nine or less) has Christ made to you?

Praying with the Church

Father, source of life,
you know our weakness.
May we reach out with joy to grasp your hand
and walk more readily in your ways.
We ask this through our Lord Jesus Christ, your Son,
who lives and reigns with You and the Holy Spirit,
one God, for ever and ever.

SATURDAY of the FOURTH WEEK of LENT
John 7:40–53

A POPULAR PORTRAIT of Jesus in our day shows him laughing. Such an interpretation might offend the serious minded; surely it would offend the Pharisees and their ilk. But Jesus, busy about his prophetic work of proclaiming the kingdom and doing the will of God, was often bemused by the strange behavior of foe and friend. It was a bemusement grounded in love and colored by compassion.

Refrain: "Never before has anyone spoken like this man."

AND JESUS LAUGHED

In himself he laughed, loving the children of men
and seeing beyond their brave follies.
There was this man Nicodemus, coming at night
and talking of two conceptions
and afraid of the wind, the Spirit
that blows wherever it wills.
And the woman, she was the bold one,
prating of her forefather Jacob
and the well water meant for his children.
He laughed in himself when unblushing
she admitted to five husbands
and said to her people, "All I have done this man knows."

But it was the Apostles he loved who most amused him.
Above all there was Peter,
rash and onrushing Peter.
He would never forget when the man stood on water,
half-naked on water, walking it,
proud of his courage,

and the terror that dashed him
when the first doubt struck him.
And then there was John the tender,
fearful and faithful.
It was he who cried, not once but three times:
"I was the first at the tomb where the Master
was laid and rose from."

Brother Edward Seifert, F.S.C.

We come to know Jesus as he interacts with the forthright Nicodemus, the well-woman with her many husbands, the impetuous
Peter, the swift-running John. It is easy to miss the laughter
in the heart of Jesus because of the seriousness of his redemptive mission. But humor and incongruity there was — and is, in
our lives.

Someone once said that laughter causes an expansion of the
heart and is thus a religious experience. I'm not sure either of
the physiology or theology of this observation, but I think it is
probably correct. Jesus' heart was expansive, embracing everyone
where they were. His experience of God came in the mutual love
between himself and the people.

1. What role does laughter play in your life? Minor or major
   actor?

2. What characters in the Gospel make you laugh?

3. What in your life bemuses God?

Praying with the Church

Lord,
guide us in your gentle mercy, for left to ourselves,
we cannot do your will.
Grant this through our Lord Jesus Christ, your Son,
who lives and reigns with You and the Holy Spirit,
one God, for ever and ever.

FIFTH WEEK OF LENT

‍

FIFTH SUNDAY of LENT

John 11:1–45 (A); John 12:20–33 (B);
John 8:1–11 (C)

JESUS met many people on his journey: Lazarus, brother of his dear friends Mary and Martha; Philip, who was without guile and a searcher after truth; the adulterous woman who knew the anger of men and the mercy of God. On our Lenten journey we too meet many individuals who shape our days: friends with whom we break bread; co-workers struggling to live responsible lives; strangers who may well disguise the Lord himself. We should pray anew for that special grace so evident in the life of Jesus: hospitality. If our hearts are open we may encounter the living and true God in surprising ways.

Refrain: "Our friend Lazarus has fallen asleep; let us go and wake him."

THE JOURNEY

And if you go up that way, you will meet with a man,
Leading a horse, whose eyes declare:
There is no God. Take no notice.

There will be other roads and other men
With the same creed, whose lips yet utter
Friendlier greeting, men who have learned
To pack a little of the sun's light
In their cold eyes, whose hands are waiting
For your hand. But do not linger.
A smile is payment; the road runs on
With many turnings towards the tall
Tree to which the believer is nailed.

R. S. Thomas

Atheism abounds. We hear it over and over, if not in word then by lifestyle, "there is no God." We are autonomous beings living on a planet that is lost in the cosmos. We are products of some mindless, evolutionary process that contains no ultimate meaning. Absurdity is the offspring of atheism.

The agnostic on the road doesn't have enough confidence to deny God and so yields to doubt. Cold eyes do give off some light and the heart hungers for compassion. Yet no faith burns here, and we are left with ambiguity and apprehension.

Farther down the road there is a tree upon which hangs a Love for all humankind. Though a cry of abandonment sounds forth, we perceive a brilliant light shining in the darkness. History tells us that all roads run to Rome; grace tells us that all journeys lead to Calvary and beyond.

1. Whom do you journey with on the road of life?

2. What is your path (lifestyle) that takes you to Calvary?

3. Do all believers get nailed to a tree?

Praying with the Church

Father,
help us to be like Christ your Son,
who loved the world and died for our salvation.
Inspire us by his love,
guide us by his example,
who lives and reigns with you and the Holy Spirit,
one God, for ever and ever.

MONDAY of the FIFTH WEEK of LENT
John 8:12–20

T HE DANGER of throwing stones at the sins of others is well known. None of us is guiltless. We all have our sins, public and hidden. Jesus, in infinite patience, refuses to condemn even the guilty. He came to bring life, life to the full, and to make people aware of their graced hidden treasure. And with the fullness of life comes peace, a peace no one can take away.

Refrain: "Whoever follows me does not walk in the dark; he will have the light of life."

HIDDEN TREASURE

Make peace with pain.
Its coming, stealthy or sudden,
is certain as winter's sunset.

A chosen companion on our lifetime journey,
entrusted with blessed task to do.

Make friends with pain.
Embrace its searing scalpel touch
waiting to mine a cross of gold
buried deep within and waiting
your choice of fuller, richer life.

Sr. Maria Corona Crumback, I.H.M.

The pain in life, be it physical, psychological or spiritual, can be redemptive or destructive. As Redeemer, Jesus meets us in our brokenness and sin, drawing us into fullness of life. At times we are dragged into his presence by public sin. At times we come under the darkness of night to seek forgiveness and healing.

Pain and suffering have their tasks to do. Whether or not we experience them as blessed depends upon the experience of peace. The woman caught in adultery suffered at many levels; the peace she experienced in meeting Christ was also multi-dimensional. Safety, acceptance, and forgiveness led her to a fuller, richer life.

1. How do you make peace with pain?

2. How does Jesus draw you into a fuller, richer life?

3. What is your hidden treasure?

Praying with the Church

Father of love, source of all blessings,
help us to pass from our old life of sin
to the new life of grace.
Prepare us for the glory of your kingdom.
We ask this through our Lord Jesus Christ, your Son,
who lives and reigns with You and the Holy Spirit,
one God, for ever and ever.

TUESDAY of the FIFTH WEEK of LENT
John 8:21–30

L ENT is a time to reflect upon and pray over our relationship with God. This involves a renewed understanding of truth, freedom, and faith. Jesus teaches only that we learn from the Father (truth); Jesus does also what pleases the Father (freedom); Jesus leads us to faith. Inseparable are truth/freedom from faith. All of nature clearly knows this.

Refrain: "When you have lifted up the Son of Man, says the Lord, you will know that I am he."

FREEDOM

Wintered bud,
tight, closed, hard.
A smooth, brown knob of stillness
resting on a barren limb,
dark, cold, alone.

Let go!
Uncurl your clutching fingerhold,
release the swelling beauty
prisoned in your grasp.

The miracle is waiting with the spring.
The giving will be graced by sun
and rich, the reward.

Sr. Maria Corona Crumback, I.H.M

Freedom is hard to come by. We cling to old patterns of thought; we get into ruts that imprison us in comforting behavior; we retain habits of the heart that contract rather than expand our love.

Jesus comes to set us free by teaching us to do all that the Father taught him. The paradox of freedom lies in our being obedient to God's will.

Freedom is like the winter bud breaking forth into fullness of life. When present, beauty and goodness are sure to follow. The Pharisees did not understand Jesus because they were not free, they did not see goodness and beauty that flowed from Jesus' words and deeds. They could not, would not, let go and life passed them by.

1. What imprisons you?

2. Make a list of three or four key moments of freedom on your journey.

3. How do you help others to be free?

Praying with the Church

Lord,
help us to do your will
that your Church may grow
and become more faithful in your service.
Grant this through our Lord Jesus Christ, your Son,
who lives and reigns with You and the Holy Spirit,
one God, for ever and ever.

WEDNESDAY of the FIFTH WEEK of LENT
John 8:31–42

L EARNING THE TRUTH that sets us free is a long journey. Often we think we know; often we claim a freedom that does not exist. When confronted with our ignorance or enslavement we deny it and attack the challenger. But then, in quiet reflection, we realize that seeing in faith alone can truly liberate us from the anxieties of life. Jesus did come to set us free.

Refrain: "If you are faithful to my teaching, says the Lord, you will indeed be my disciples. You will know the truth and the truth will make you free."

ONLY HE WHO SEES
(For Sr. Marie St. Catherine, R.I.P.)

"Life is a mystery to be lived,
Not a problem to be solved."

So wrote the French philosopher.

What gift to help us bear our awful watch
before this bright young spirit
slowly yielding to a ravaging foe
creeping on with deadly stealth.
Waiting, too, can crush the heart!

Instead, with lifted faith,
we look for silent strength
at the cross close upon her wall —
the paradox of love-in-pain —
and know that, somehow, this oblation
is enfolded by Divinity.

God, gift our vision with Your grace,
still our all-too-human "Why?"
that before such awesome mystery,
we who weep
may humbly "take off our shoes"
and adore.

Sr. Maria Corona Crumback, I.H.M.

Life is both a mystery and a problem. Incomprehensible are the actions of grace in the mysteries of creation, redemption, sanctification; overwhelming are the problems of evil, suffering, and death. Our truth, the truth that sets us free, lies in the paradoxical cross that embraces the contradictions of life: sin and grace, hate and love, death and life.

Jesus invites us to faith, to that radical conviction that God is faithful to the divine promises. This fidelity can almost, yet not totally, remove our "whys." This fidelity empowers us to bend the knee in adoration because we have seen the presence of God in the burning bush, in the death of a loved one, in the movements of the heart.

1. Is life more a problem or a mystery for you?

2. What makes you "take off your shoes"?

3. How has your theology of the cross grown over the years?

Praying with the Church

Father of mercy,
hear the prayers of your repentant children
who call on you in love.
Enlighten our minds and sanctify our hearts.

We ask this through our Lord Jesus Christ, your Son,
who lives and reigns with You and the Holy Spirit,
one God, for ever and ever.

THURSDAY of the FIFTH WEEK of LENT
John 8:51–59

J ESUS LIVED in intimate friendship with the Father. His mission
was to lead others into a relationship characterized by peace
and joy. But some people had staked out territories of power and
prestige, of authority and self-righteousness. They were not open
to the full revelation of God given in Jesus. Proof of all this was
manifest in the killing of those who spoke the truth — Jesus and
all the other prophets. Yet Jesus extends the gift of friendship to
all, indeed, to us this day.

Refrain: "Jesus said to the chief priests and the crowds of the
Jews: Whoever comes from God hears the word of God. You will
not listen because you do not come from God."

FRIENDSHIP

There are minds that meet
and slowly match in thought
until they merge in
communion.

There are hearts that meet
and slowly blend
as the Lord's own in
communion.

There are souls that meet
and, together, search
for peace and truth in
communion.

Rare the gift, but blessed
are those who share in
mind,
          heart, and
                    soul,
Communion.

Sr. Maria Corona Crumback, I.H.M.

Friendship and community are about communion, a coming together in mind and heart. Fullness of life depends upon the experience of union with God and unity within the human family. Jesus came to unify us, to save us, to redeem us. His mission flowed from his communion with the Father.

Happy are those who know friendship. How rare this gift is, who's to say? Surely the gift is offered in abundance, how else explain the universality of grace? Yet it is in the reception of the gift that the problem lies. Open hearts, open minds is the Lenten grace we need.

1. Who are your friends?

2. How would you describe your friendship with God?

3. To whom have you extended the gift of friendship?

Praying with the Church

Lord,
come to us;
free us from the stain of sin.
Help us to remain faithful to a holy way of life,
and guide us to the inheritance you promised.
Grant this through our Lord Jesus Christ, your Son,
who lives and reigns with You and the Holy Spirit,
one God, for ever and ever.

FRIDAY of the FIFTH WEEK of LENT
John 10:31–42

J ESUS IS THE LIGHT of the nations. The work the Father gave him to do was to enlighten the minds and hearts of people with the truth. Some people recognized Jesus as Lord and believed. Others, caught in semantics and blindness, did not see and would not believe. They continued the darkness of the world by gathering stones to destroy the innocent one. They refused to do the work God intended for them.

Refrain: "The Lord said: I have done you many acts of kindness; for which of these do you want to kill me?"

A Candle

"I lit a candle and prayed," you wrote.
A promised pause in your pilgrimage
another world away.

As taper tip touched candle wick,
it danced a bit, then settled down
to burn, as candles do,
its flickering life of prayer.

But the glow. Ah, the glow!
Flamed across an ocean
and shone across my day,
dark with care,
like a steady, sure, and shining star.

And the warm embrace
of love in Christ
lifted my eyes to the hills again.

Go, dear pilgrim, on your way.
While here and there,
as you light a candle
and say a prayer,
my heart keeps watch in thankfulness
and knows the gift:

That in the night
the stars will shine again.

Sr. Maria Corona Crumback, I.H.M.

We are a pilgrim people. On this long journey of life there are
few things more important than bringing light to the darkness.
We light our candles and fear scatters; we profess our love and

hate wanes; we offer hope and spring comes once again into the human heart. Our candles and prayers are graces for the journey.

Still the night is with us. We do live by faith, not by sight. Two things are necessary if we are to remain faithful to our call to discipleship: prayer and love. In prayer, the darkness is challenged; in love, the promise of dawn is realized.

1. How does prayer bring light to our world?

2. In what sense are we pilgrims with Christ?

3. How do you deal with the night experiences of life?

Praying with the Church

Lord,
grant us your forgiveness,
and set us free from our enslavement to sin.
We ask this through our Lord Jesus Christ, your Son,
who lives and reigns with You and the Holy Spirit,
one God, for ever and ever.

SATURDAY of the FIFTH WEEK of LENT
John 11:45–57

IN SETTING his face toward Jerusalem, Jesus did so for one reason: to fulfill the will of God. The meaning of the cross lies in the purpose of redemption: gathering all creation back to God. The paradox and contradictions of the cross test our faith. We must keep our focus on the Lord lest we lose our way.

Refrain: "Jesus died to gather into one family all the scattered children of God."

COMFORT
(For Carolyn, my only postulant)

Fear not, young heart,
the Calvary road,
though rough it be and far.
Let not the sting
of biting wind
bedim your glowing star.

For God Himself
will be your strength;
His peace, your pain repay.
And there will be Veronicas
and Simons on the way.

Sr. Maria Corona Crumback, I.H.M.

The choice to walk the Calvary road, i.e., the road of discipleship, necessarily is a choice to participate in the cross of Christ. Though the way be rough and the wind biting, there are deep consolations: God's strength, God's peace, God's special messengers. We do not travel alone.

Yet young and old hearts are fearful. We need but spend a moment in Gethsemane to know that the Master himself was sorely tested. The angels that ministered to him also come to us. The Veronicas and Simons bring God's peace.

1. Who are the Veronicas and Simons in your life?

2. How do you deal with fear, the fear of suffering on the cross?

3. How does God strengthen you these Lenten days?

Praying with the Church

God our Father,
you always wish to save us,
and now we rejoice in the great love
you gave to your chosen people.
Protect all who are about to become your children,
and continue to bless those who are already baptized.
Grant this through our Lord Jesus Christ, your Son,
who lives and reigns with You and the Holy Spirit,
one God, for ever and ever.

HOLY WEEK

⚜

PASSION SUNDAY (Palm Sunday)
Matthew 26:14–27:66 (A); Mark 14:1–15:47 (B);
Luke 22:14–23:56 (C)

THE PASSION NARRATIVE stirs up a multitude of feelings: shame for sin, guilt for our betrayals, joy in the gift of Eucharist, gratitude for the mystery of redemption. Each year the liturgy draws us into the paschal mystery which, if tasted deeply, fashions our hearts and deepens our love. The Good Friday events of betrayal and death drive home the cost of discipleship and the realism of the Gospel message. Life demands death; love requires self-donation; mercy necessitates divine compassion.

Refrain: "With palms let us welcome the Lord as he comes, with songs and hymns let us run to meet him, as we offer him our joyful worship and sing: Blessed be the Lord!"

GOOD FRIDAY

It was quiet. What had the sentry
to cry, but that it was the ninth hour
and all was not well? The darkness
began to lift, but it was not the mind

was illumined. The carpenter
had done his work well to sustain

the carpenter's burden; the Cross an example
of the power of art to transcend timber.

R. S. Thomas

All is not well. War, hatred, racism dehumanize our human existence causing immense suffering and anguish. Jesus entered into
this human condition. Before *the* Good Friday, there were other
days of self-emptying. Jesus came that we might have the fullness
of life even if that meant he must die.

With death comes darkness, the darkness of the tomb and the
darkness that penetrates the human mind. We become confused
when those we love die. Lacking personal experience, we do not
know what lies beyond our last breath nor the last breath of those
we love. And what a darkness it is even if faith is strong.

At the center of Good Friday is the cross, the symbol of love
and sin. Some carpenter did the work, not realizing how art and
its rich symbolism transcend our limited human meanings. Timber we can feel and cut; the Love nailed to the tree remains too
deep for our comprehension. We kneel before the mystery in the
quiet and pain of Good Friday.

1. What happens in your heart when you read the passion
   story?

2. How do you deal with the "all is not well" of life?

3. How do you reverence the cross?

Praying with the Church

Almighty, ever-living God,
you have given the human race Jesus Christ our Savior
as a model of humility.
He fulfilled your will
by becoming man and giving his life on the cross.

Help us to bear witness to you
by following his example of suffering
and make us worthy to share his resurrection.
We ask this through our Lord Jesus Christ, your Son,
who lives and reigns with you and the Holy Spirit,
one God, for ever and ever.

MONDAY of HOLY WEEK
John 12:1–11

As we step into Holy Week we must be prepared to participate ever more deeply in the agony of our Lord's sacrificial
death. The events can be overly familiar, the story too well
known. Prayer and penance are necessary if we are to taste deeply
the betrayal of Judas, the compassion and love of Mary, the terror of Jesus, the constant talk of murder and death. Yet in all
of this, salvation is at hand. God's giving is extravagant; God's
mercy, everlasting.

Refrain: "Father, Righteous One, the world does not know you,
but I know you, because you are the One who sent me."

The Second Giving

The second giving of God is the great giving
out of the portions of the seraphim,
abundances with which the soul is laden
once it has given up all things for Him.

The second growth of God is the rich growing,
with fruits no constant gathering can remove,
the flourishing of those who by God's mercy
have cut themselves down to the roots for love.

God seeks a heart with bold and boundless hungers
that sees itself and earth as paltry stuff;
God loves a soul that cast down all He gave it
and stands and cries that it was not enough.

Jessica Powers

God does seek bold and boundless hearts like Peter and Paul. God has a special love for generous souls that simply cannot give enough back to an abundant Deity, like Mary and Martha. God loves his Son who offers everything in return to save humankind.

Judas could not stand such generosity since it was a judgment on his paltry love. More, as a betrayer and thief, he attempted to block others from making an extravagant return to God. Sin hates grace; darkness dreads light; hardness of heart thwarts compassion. Jesus accepts Mary's gesture of love that prepares him for his ultimate sacrifice.

1. How do you anoint the Lord's feet?

2. What aspect of Judas's life are reflected in your own?

3. How are you preparing yourself for the great Easter mysteries?

Praying with the Church

All powerful God,
by the suffering and death of your Son,
strengthen and protect us in our weakness.
We ask this through our Lord Jesus Christ, your Son,

who lives and reigns with You and the Holy Spirit,
one God, for ever and ever.

TUESDAY of HOLY WEEK
John 13:21–31, 36–38

A MBIGUITY characterizes life. Weather is fair and foul; crops abundant and scarce; people glorious and tragic. The glory of Jesus flows out of his faithful obedience in laying down his life for the redemption of the world. The tragedy of humankind is the ignominy of disobedience, betrayal, and cowardice. Today's Gospel manifests how wonderful and terrible the soul can be. Ambiguity characterizes life.

Refrain: "Father, give me the glory that I had with you before the world was made."

The Soul Is a Terrible Thing

The soul is a terrible thing; it cannot die.
Though it run past the heart's beat and the lung's breath
and cry through all the valleys of endlessness
it cannot find its death.

The soul is a terrible thing, and it has only
one of two destinies:
up steeps of light that to the eye below
are too remote, too lonely,
cliffs of negation where the heart's herb withers,
solitudes chilled and barren, or a deep

unknown where midnight wanders in her sleep.
Yet its ascensions open upon wonder,
plateaus of midday, balconies of sun,
and its last peak can cleave the white air under
the firmament called God, the final One.

Failing to rise, the soul can turn and follow
the way of its own willing and be lost,
crossing somewhere the boundaries of love,
that safe sweet nation of the Holy Ghost.
The soul though born of God can yet be given
to ultimate evil and be one of those
in pain alone preserved
whom the apt metaphors of Judas enclose:
wandering stars to whom the storm of darkness
is forever reserved.
Yet its true destiny confounds all language,
even the mind's profound imagined word.
For on the heights of grace it yet may be
the secret chamber of the Deity
where what is spoken in God, in God is heard.
And what is Love proceeds eternally,
possessing utterly.

Oh, at this mystery that lies within me
I walk indeed with trembling, or I stand
crying God's pities out of His right hand —
that I, so poor a creature, am so favored
with this too precious gift of soul, that I
bear in so undependable a vessel
this terrible, terrible thing they call a soul.

Jessica Powers

Two destinies stood before Judas. He chose the way of his own willing and went out into the night and took his own life. His storm of darkness terrible, his lostness severe. Somewhere, sometime Judas crossed "the boundaries of love" and sought only himself.

Two destinies stood before Peter. Impetuous, he claimed fidelity and bravery. Events did not follow his verbal designs. He too went out into the night, faced his betrayal with tears, and recommitted himself to his Lord. He walked back across the boundaries of love into Spirit's "safe sweet nation."

1. What choices are you making regarding your two destinies?

2. Do you consider your soul a terrible thing?

3. Where are the boundaries of love found in your life?

Praying with the Church

Father,
may we receive your forgiveness and mercy
as we celebrate the passion and death of the Lord,
Who lives and reigns with You and the Holy Spirit,
one God, for ever and ever.

WEDNESDAY of HOLY WEEK
Matthew 26:14–25

RIENDSHIP is built on trust. One lives with the conviction that people who are close to us and have shared life in special ways will not hurt or betray us. Yet sin touches all of our hearts. We are capable of violating trust, breaking confidences, selling friendships for thirty pieces of silver. The story of Judas Iscariot is not unfamiliar either in experience or narrative from our lives. We do well to tremble in reading the tale of a Passover betrayal.

Refrain: "Through the eternal Spirit, Christ offered himself to God as the perfect sacrifice. His blood purifies us from sin and makes us fit servants of the living God."

TAKE YOUR ONLY SON

None guessed our nearness to the land of vision,
not even our two companions to the mount.
That you bore wood and I, by grave decision,
fire and a sword, they judged of small account.

Speech might leap wide to what were best unspoken
and so we plodded, silent, through the dust.
I turned my gaze lest the heart be twice broken
when innocence looked up to smile its trust.

O love far deeper than a lone begotten,
how grievingly I let your words be lost
when a shy question guessed I had forgotten
a thing so vital as the holocaust.

Hope may shout promise of reward unending
and faith buy bells to ring its gladness thrice,

but these do not preclude earth's tragic ending
and a heart shattered in its sacrifice.

Not beside Abram does my story set me.
I built the altar, laid the wood for flame.
I stayed my sword as long as duty let me,
and then alas, alas, no angel came.

Jessica Powers

There are parallels between the story of Abraham and his son
Isaac, between God and his son Jesus. Both stories are about
sacrifice, both about the anguish of life and death. On Mount
Horeb, Isaac regained his life. On Calvary, Jesus met death. The
sword fell and the world wept.

Though similar up to a point, the Mount Horeb and Calvary
stories differ greatly. At the core of the crucifixion is betrayal. The
Messiah is sold for thirty pieces of silver while his betrayer re-
clines with him at table. Judas Iscariot breaks trust with the Lord
who loved him.

1. Why is a sin carried to a family table so horrendous?

2. What types of betrayal take place in our times?

3. What does the Passover meal mean to you?

Praying with the Church

Father,
in your plan of salvation
your Son Jesus Christ accepted the cross
and freed us from the power of the enemy.
May we come to share the glory of his resurrection,
for he lives and reigns with You and the Holy Spirit,
one God, for ever and ever.

HOLY THURSDAY

John 13:1–15 — Lord's Supper

GOD'S LOVE is ritualized in a unique way on Holy Thursday. Jesus not only shares the intimacy of a meal, a last meal, with his disciples, but he gives them a simple, clear example of what discipleship is all about: service. Washing one another's feet, feeding the hungry, clothing the naked — here is the core of the Eucharist, our great miracle of love.

Refrain: "I have longed to eat this meal with you before I suffer."

THE LEFTOVERS

With twenty loaves of bread Elisha fed
the one hundred till they were satisfied,
and Scripture tells us there was bread left over.
Jesus did more: with five small barley loaves
and two dried fish he fed five thousand men,
together with their wives and children, all
neatly arranged upon the cushioned grass.
The awed disciples, when the crowd had eaten,
gathered up what was left: twelve baskets full.

Who then received these fragments? Hopefully,
the least (though not less favored) and the poor.
I think of those who always seem to get
the leavings from the banqueting of others,
the scraps of bread, of life, that goodness saves.
I pray that they come proudly when invited,
make merry at their meal and have their fill,
and rise up thankfully, remembering
the fragments, too, were miracles of love.

Jessica Powers

God's table is large, as large as creation. All are invited, all are to have access to the necessity of food and the miracle of love. Both are essential to the fullness of life. Without food, the body languishes and dies; without love, our souls wither and are filled with despair.

The leftovers in our lives? What are they and who will get them? So many people can live off our leavings if we would only share. This is hardly sufficient. Disciples of Christ give abundantly in imitation of the Master who gave his very self.

1. Whom do you invite to your table?

2. When did you last experience the miracle of love?

3. Who are "the least" and "the poor" in your life?

Praying with the Church

> God of infinite compassion,
> to love you is to be made holy;
> fill our hearts with your love.
> By the death of your Son
> you have given us hope, born of faith;
> by his rising again
> fulfilled his hope
> in the perfect love of heaven,
> where he lives and reigns with You and the Holy Spirit,
> one God, for ever and ever.

GOOD FRIDAY
John 18:1–19, 42

I N READING the account of the mystery of redemption, our faith is put to the test. Salvation coming through the cross? Life recovered through death? Our God crucified? Unless the Spirit enlightens our hearts we will remain in the darkness of doubt. Come, Holy Spirit, come!

Refrain: "Over his head there hung the accusation: Jesus of Nazareth, King of the Jews."

CHRIST IS MY UTMOST NEED

Late, late the mind confessed:
wisdom has not sufficed.
I cannot take one step into the light
without the Christ.

Late, late the heart affirmed:
wild do my heart-beats run
when in the blood-stream sings one wish away
from the Incarnate Son.

Christ is my utmost need.
I lift each breath, each beat for Him to bless,
knowing our language cannot overspeak
our frightening helplessness.

Here where proud morning walks
and we hang wreaths on power and self-command,
I cling with all my strength unto a nail-
investigated hand.

Christ is my only trust.
I am my fear since, down the lanes of ill,

my steps surprised a dark Iscariot
plotting in my own will.

Past nature called, I cry
who clutch at fingers and at tunic folds,
"lay not on me, O Christ, this fastening.
Yours be the hand that holds."

Jessica Powers

Our needs in life are many: the need for food and drink; the need
for belonging and affection; the need for salvation. Our minds
confess and hearts affirm that Christ is our utmost need, for without his redemptive presence our helplessness turns into despair. It
is his hands that hold us and give us salvation.

Too often we trust, not in the saving cross of Christ, but in
power, self-command, prestige — even virtue. None of these can
save. None of these can overcome our radical poverty. Our confidence and faith must be grounded in a God who became one of
us, suffered and died, rose from the dead that we might have life,
life to the full.

1. Make a list of your needs! Where is Christ on that list?

2. Does a dark Iscariot dwell in your will?

3. Why is even wisdom insufficient in this life?

Praying with the Church
Father,
look with love upon your people,
the love which our Lord Jesus Christ showed us
when he delivered himself to evil men
and suffered the agony of the cross,
for he lives and reigns with You and the Holy Spirit,
one God, for ever and ever.

HOLY SATURDAY NIGHT, EASTER VIGIL
Matthew 28:1–10

C HRIST IS THE LIGHT of the world. The Gospel dispels our darkness, enabling us to come to a new self-understanding. It is a Gospel filled with paradox: obedience giving freedom, death bringing forth life; suffering leading to infinite joy. And we are invited to participate in this divine comedy, this heavenly race, this great mystery of love and mercy.

Refrain: "For our sake Christ was obedient, accepting even death, death on a cross. Therefore God raised him on high and gave him a name above all other names."

EVERYTHING RUSHES, RUSHES

The brisk blue morning whisked in with a thought:
everything in creation rushes, rushes
toward God — tall trees, small bushes,
quick birds and fish, the beetles round as naught,

eels in the water, deer on forest floor,
what sits in trees, what burrows underground,
what wriggles to declare life must abound,
and we, the spearhead that run on before,

and lesser things to which life cannot come:
our work, our words that move toward the Unmoved,
whatever can be touched, used, handled, loved —
all, all are rushing on *ad terminum.*

So I, with eager voice and news-flushed face,
cry to those caught in comas, stupors, sleeping:

come, everything is running
>   flying,
>   leaping,
>   hurtling through time!
>   And we are in this race.

Jessica Powers

The great mysteries of our faith: creation, covenant, incarnation, redemption, resurrection, Pentecost! And all of us are participants in the race of grace, coming from God and rushing back into the divine presence. The Easter vigil gives us a sense of urgency as people hurry to and from an empty tomb.

We must shake off our comas and stupors and lazy sleeping. We must arise and go with the risen Lord toward the fullness of light and peace. Time and eternity intersect; finitude and infinity lose their boundaries. All creation is gathered to a great oneness — now!

1. What is your sense of urgency regarding God's kingdom?

2. What comas and stupors do you have to deal with?

3. Is your voice eager and is your face ever flushed?

Praying with the Church

All powerful and ever loving God,
your only Son went down among the dead
and rose again in glory.

In your goodness
raise up your faithful people,
buried with him in baptism,
to be one with him
in the eternal life of heaven,
where he lives and reigns with You and the Holy Spirit
one God, for ever and ever.

EASTER

༺╬༻

EASTER SUNDAY
John 20:1–9

A NEW PRESENCE was felt by those who, just a few days before, saw their Master crucified. A new presence, mysterious but real, that pressed in upon their souls with joy and a disturbing peace. The bonds of death broken. Life won the day. The Easter mystery transformed lives and confirmed love. Now all was new. A light shone in the darkness, never to be extinguished. And though all creation an eternal alleluia echoed and re-echoed.

Refrain: "Very early on the morning after the Sabbath, when the sun had just risen, they came to the tomb, alleluia."

THE PRESENCE

I pray and incur
silence. Some take that silence
for refusal.
            I feel the power
that, invisible, catches me
by the sleeve, nudging
            towards the long shelf

that has the book on it I will take down
   and read and find the antidote
to an ailment.
   I know its ways with me;
how it enters my life,
   is present rather
before I perceive it, sunlight quivering
on a bare wall.
   Is it consciousness trying
to get through?
   Am I under
regard?
   It takes me seconds
to focus, by which time
   it has shifted its gaze,
looking a little to one
   side, as though I were not here.

It has the universe
   to be abroad in.
There is nothing I can do
but fill myself with my own
   silence, hoping it will approach
   like a wild creature to drink
there, or perhaps like Narcissus
to linger a moment over its transparent face.

          R. S. Thomas

Silence in the soul, songs on the lips. Easter is the experience
of a new, majestic presence of the Christ. As light scatters the
darkness of death, so love leads to the fullness of life. The power
of grace grabs us by the sleeve and leads us to an empty tomb,
invites us to the banquet of joy.

Easter assures us that we are under regard, that God's promise of presence is fulfilled. We are neither abandoned nor lost in
the universe. Rather, the risen Christ, now disguised as a pilgrim,
gardener, cook continues to visit humankind with compassion
and mercy. We are under regard. We cry out, alleluia.

The entire universe is filled with a new presence. Every nation
and people, every home and city can experience this divine vis-
itation. In the silence we encounter grace. In openness of heart,
we surrender to life. In abandonment to the will of God, we find
peace.

1. Is Easter a time of silence or singing?

2. How do you make people feel they are under regard?

3. How do you experience the Easter presence of the risen
   Lord?

Praying with the Church

God our Father,
by raising Christ, your Son,
you conquered the power of death
and opened for us the way to eternal life.
Let our celebration today
raise us up and renew our lives
by the Spirit that is within us.
Grant this through our Lord Jesus Christ, your Son,
who lives and reigns with you and the Holy Spirit,
one God, for ever and ever.

CONCLUSION

The journey from Ash Wednesday to Easter Sunday is a long and arduous one. But we do not travel alone. Poets, prophets and mystics are our guides. So too our sisters and brothers in the Lord with whom we share the joys and sorrows of our faith. But there a special companion, a mentor and model who lived fully the paschal mystery, Mary, the mother of Jesus, the mother of the Church, and our mother.

This Lenten meditation began with a poem on Mary as "The Handmaid." Please reread that verse and ponder again "Is this the way it was...?"

There is no better way to conclude these reflections than by returning to the Annunciation story, the turning point of history. Again we can seek the guidance of a poet, this time a truly surprising one, Edgar Allan Poe. His hymn to Mary is a fitting prayer to continuing our journey into "ordinary time."

Hymn

At morn — at noon — at twilight dim —
Maria! thou hast heard my hymn!
In joy and woe — in good and ill —
Mother of God, be with me still!
When the Hours flew brightly by,
And not a cloud obscured the sky,
My soul, lest it should truant be,
Thy grace did guide to thine and thee;
Now, when storms of Fate o'ercast
Darkly my Present and my Past,
Let my Future radiant shine
With sweet hopes of thee and thine!

Acknowledgments

Scripture quotations are from the New Revised Standard Version Bible, © 1989 by Division of Christian Education of the National Council of the Churches of Christ in the United States of America.

"The Sculpture," "The Handmaid," "Hidden Treasure," "Freedom," "Only He Who Sees," "Friendship," "A Candle," "Comfort," from *Gift Fragments*, by Sr. Maria Corona Crumback, I.H.M., published by Sheed & Ward, Kansas City, Missouri, © 1989 Carmelite Monastery of Pewaukee, Wisconsin. "Hidden Treasure" first appeared in *Review for Religious* 52 (1993): 460.

"The Master Beggar," "The Sign of the Cross," "The Masses," "Heaven," "The Second Giving," "The Soul Is a Terrible Thing," "Take Your Only Son," "The Leftovers," "Christ Is My Utmost Need," "Everything Rushes, Rushes," from *Selected Poetry of Jessica Powers*, edited by Regina Siegfried, A.S.C., and Robert F. Morneau. Used by permission of Sheed & Ward, 115 E. Armour Blvd., Kansas City, MO 64141. To order, call (800)333-7373.

"The Moor," "In Church," "The Letter," "The Kingdom," "The Journey," "Good Friday," "The Presence," from *Poems of R. S. Thomas*, 1985, © R. S. Thomas reprinted with permission of the University of Arkansas Press, Fayetteville, Arkansas.

"Redemption," "Prayer (I)," "A Wreath," "The Pulley," "Love (III)," "Matins," from *George Herbert: The Country Parson, the Temple*, ed. John N. Wall, Jr., © 1981 by The Missionary Society of St. Paul the Apostle in the State of New York. Used by Permission of Paulist Press.

"A Saint," "Lyrics for the Christian," "Invitation," "How Weary the Road," "The Wonder of Good," "Gospel Celebrities," from *Exploration into God: New and Collected Poems*, by Gordon Gilsdorf, published by Alt Publishing Company, Green Bay, Wisconsin, © 1992 by Gordon Gilsdorf.

"Mother Teresa," "The Tassel of His Cloak," "Death, Luminous Death," "God Is Not Nice," "He Spoke of Christ," "And Jesus Laughed," by Brother Edward Seifert, F.S.C., from *Gift, Mystery, and Calling: Prayers and Reflections*, featuring the poetry of Brother Edward Seifert, F.S.C., © 1994 by St. Mary's Press, Christian Brothers Publications, Winona, Minnesota.